MW00562232

# みんなの日本語 初級II 第2版

# Minna no Nihongo

Elementary Japanese II
Translation & Grammar Notes–English

## 翻訳・文法解説 英語版

スリーエーネットワーク

Published by 3A Corporation.
Trusty Kojimachi Bldg., 2F, 4, Kojimachi 3-Chome, Chiyoda-ku, Tokyo 102-0083, Japan

ISBN978-4-88319-664-7 C0081

First published 1998
Second Edition 2013
Printed in Japan

# FOREWORD

As the title ***Minna no Nihongo*** indicates, this book has been designed to make the study of Japanese as enjoyable and interesting as possible for students and teachers alike. Over three years in the planning and compilation, it stands as a complete textbook in itself while acting as a companion volume to the highly-regarded ***Shin Nihongo no Kiso***.

As readers may know, ***Shin Nihongo no Kiso*** is a comprehensive introduction to elementary Japanese that serves as a highly efficient resource enabling students wishing to master basic Japanese conversation to do so in the shortest possible time. As such, although it was originally developed for use by AOTS's technical trainees, it is now used by a wide range of people both in Japan and abroad.

The teaching of Japanese is branching out in many different ways. Japanese economic and industrial growth has led to a greater level of interchange between Japan and other countries, and non-Japanese from a wide variety of backgrounds have come to Japan with a range of different objectives and are now living within local communities here. The changes in the social milieu surrounding the teaching of Japanese that have resulted from this influx of people from other countries have in turn influenced the individual situations in which Japanese is taught. There is now a greater diversity of learning needs, and they require individual responses.



It is against this background, and in response to the opinions and hopes expressed by a large number of people who have been involved in the teaching of Japanese for many years both in Japan and elsewhere, that 3A Corporation proudly publishes ***Minna no Nihongo***. While the book continues to make use of the clarity and ease of understanding provided by the special features, key learning points and learning methods of ***Shin Nihongo no Kiso***, the scenes, situations and characters in ***Minna no Nihongo*** have been made more universal in order to appeal to a wider range of learners. Its contents have been enhanced in this way to allow all kinds of students to use it for studying Japanese with pleasure.

***Minna no Nihongo*** is aimed at anyone who urgently needs to learn to communicate in Japanese in any situation, whether at work, school, college or in their local community. Although it is an introductory text, efforts have been made to make the exchanges between Japanese and foreign characters in the book reflect Japanese social conditions and everyday life as faithfully as possible. While it is intended principally for those who have already left full-time education, it can also be recommended as an excellent textbook for university entrance courses as well as for short-term intensive courses at technical colleges and universities.

We at 3A Corporation are continuing actively to produce new study materials designed to meet the individual needs of an increasingly wide range of learners, and we sincerely hope that readers will continue to give us their valued support.

In conclusion, I should like to mention the extensive help we received in the preparation of this text, in the form of suggestions and comments from various quarters, and trials of the materials in actual lessons, for which we are extremely grateful. 3A Corporation intends to continue extending its network of friendship all over the world through activities such as the publishing of Japanese study materials, and we hope that everyone who knows us will continue to lend us their unstinting encouragement and support in this.

Iwao Ogawa

President, 3A Corporation

June 1998

# FOREWORD TO THE SECOND EDITION

— On the Publication of the Second Edition of ***Minna no Nihongo Shokyu*** —

We are proud to publish the second edition of ***Minna no Nihongo Shokyu***. As stated in the Foreword to the first edition, ***Minna no Nihongo Shokyu*** can be regarded as a companion volume to ***Shin Nihongo no Kiso***, a textbook originally developed for technical trainees.

The first printing of the first edition of ***Minna no Nihongo Shokyu I*** was issued in March 1998, when great changes in the social environment surrounding the teaching of Japanese were taking place. The burgeoning of relationships between Japan and the rest of the world had led to a rapid increase in the number of students of Japanese and their reasons for studying the language, and the consequent diversification of their requirements had necessitated a response more tailored to learners' individual situations. 3A Corporation published ***Minna no Nihongo Shokyu*** in response to suggestions and comments received from people on the front lines of Japanese teaching in Japan and elsewhere.

***Minna no Nihongo Shokyu*** was acclaimed for its easily-understood key learning points and methods, its high degree of general applicability that took into account learners' diversity, and for being a carefully-crafted learning resource that was outstandingly effective for students attempting to master Japanese conversation quickly. It has served well for over ten years, but any language changes with the times, and both Japan and other countries have experienced great upheavals recently. Particularly in the last few years, the environment in which the Japanese language and its learners are situated has changed drastically.

In these circumstances, 3A Corporation decided to review and partially revise ***Minna no Nihongo Shokyu I*** and ***II***, based on our publishing and training experience and reflecting the many opinions and questions we have received from students and teachers of Japanese, in order to be able to contribute further to the teaching of Japanese as a foreign language.

The revision focused on making the book even more usable and changing any words or scenarios that no longer reflected current conditions. Respecting the wishes of students and teachers, we have preserved the original textbook format, which has the benefit of making the book easy to use for both learning and teaching, and we have introduced more exercises and practice questions designed to strengthen students' active language ability by inviting them to understand situations for themselves and think about how to express themselves, rather than merely following instructions and practising in a passive way. We have included a large number of illustrations for this purpose.

We are extremely grateful for the enormous help we received in the editing of this book, in the form of comments and suggestions from various quarters, and trials in actual lessons. 3A Corporation intends to continue developing textbooks that can not only help students of Japanese to communicate what they need to but also contribute to international interpersonal interchange, and we hope that everyone engaged in such activities will find them useful. We warmly invite everyone who knows us to continue to lend us their unstinting encouragement and support in this.

Takuji Kobayashi
President, 3A Corporation
January 2013

# TO USERS OF THIS BOOK

## Ⅰ. Structure

The second edition of ***Minna no Nihongo Shokyu II*** consists of two volumes: the Main Text (with CD) and the Translation and Grammar Notes. We plan to publish the Translation and Grammar Notes in twelve languages, starting with English.

The materials have been compiled with the aim of inculcating the four skills of speaking, listening, reading and writing. However the Main Text and the Translation and Grammar Notes do not provide any instruction in reading and writing hiragana, katakana, or kanji.

## Ⅱ. Contents

### 1. Main Text

#### 1) Lessons

There are 25 lessons, numbered 26 to 50 (following on from Lessons 1-25 in the second edition of Minna no Nihongo Shokyu I), each containing the following:

① Sentence patterns

Basic sentence patterns to be learned in that lesson.

② Example sentences

Basic sentence patterns incorporated into short dialogues to show how they are used in actual conversation. New adverbs, conjunctions, and other parts of speech, plus further learning points, are also introduced.

③ Conversation

In the Conversation, foreign people living in Japan appear in a variety of situations. The Conversation includes everyday greetings and other expressions and as well as the material to be learned in the lesson. If time allows, students can try developing the Conversation by introducing some of the Useful Words given in the Translation and Grammar Notes.

④ Exercises

The exercises are split into three levels: A, B, and C.

Exercise A is laid out visually to help students understand the grammatical structure easily. It has been designed to make it easy for students to practise conjugating verbs and forming connections, as well as mastering the basic sentence patterns.

Exercise B employs various forms to strengthen students' grasp of the basic sentence patterns. A number with an arrow (➡) indicates an exercise that uses an illustration.

Exercise C is designed to help students improve their communication abilities. Students use this exercise to practise conversing while substituting the underlined words in the designated conversation with alternatives matching the situation; however, to prevent this becoming a simple substitution drill, students should practise with these exercises by changing the substitutable parts to match their own circumstances, expanding the subject matter, and developing the situations further.

Model answers to Exercises B and C are available in a separate compilation volume.

⑤ Practice questions

There are four types of practice question: Listening Comprehension, Grammar, Reading Comprehension, and Topics for Development. The Listening Comprehension Questions are further subdivided into two types: answering short questions, and listening to short conversations and grasping the key points. The Grammar Questions check students' understanding of vocabulary and grammar points. For the Reading Comprehension exercises, students read a passage incorporating previously-studied words and grammar, and perform various linguistic tasks related to its subject matter. For the Topics for Development, they write and talk about topics related to the passages. In Minna no Nihongo Shokyu II, the Reading Comprehension passages are written without spaces in order to gradually accustom intermediate-level students to the normal style of Japanese writing, although spaces are used elsewhere in the texts for educational purposes.



⑥ Review

This is provided to enable students to go over the essential points once more every few lessons.

⑦ Summary of Adverbs, Conjunctions and Conversational Expressions

These are practice questions designed to enable students to review the adverbs, conjunctions and conversational expressions presented in this textbook.

**2) Verb forms**

This section summarises the verb forms presented in this textbook (including Shokyu I), together with various forms added to the ends of verbs.

**3) Table of Key Learning Points**

This is a summary of the key learning points presented in this textbook, focusing on Exercise A. It indicates which of the Sentence Patterns, Example Sentences, and Exercises B and C are relevant to each of the learning points introduced in Exercise A.

**4) Index**

The Index includes all new words and phrases introduced in Lessons 1 through 50, together with the number of the lesson in which they first appear.

### 5) Included CD

The CD that goes with this book contains the Conversation and the Listening Comprehension exercises from each lesson.

## 2. Translation and Grammar notes

These consist of the following for each of Lessons 26 through 50:

① New words and their translations.

② Translations of Sentence Patterns, Example Sentences and Conversations.

③ Useful words relevant to each lesson and snippets of information on Japan.

④ Explanations of the grammar of the Sentence Patterns and expressions.

# Ⅲ. Time Required to Complete the Lessons

As a guideline, it should take students 4-6 hours to cover each lesson, and 150 hours to finish the entire book.

# Ⅳ. Vocabulary

The book presents approximately 1,000 words, mainly ones used frequently in daily life.

# Ⅴ. Kanji Usage

Wherever possible, kanji used in this book have been selected from the list of Kanji for Regular Use (Joyo Kanji) announced by the Japanese Cabinet in 1981.

**1)** 熟字訓 (じゅくじくん) (words that are formed from two or more kanji and have a special reading) which appear in the Appendix to the Joyo Kanji list are written in kanji:

e.g. 友達 (ともだち) friend　果物 (くだもの) fruit　眼鏡 (めがね) spectacles

**2)** Some kanji and readings not appearing in the Joyo Kanji list have been used in place names, people's names and other proper nouns, and in words from artistic, cultural and other specialised fields:

e.g. 大阪 (おおさか) Osaka　奈良 (なら) Nara　歌舞伎 (かぶき) kabuki

**3)** To make the text easier to read, some words have been written in kana even though they appear in the Joyo Kanji list:

e.g. ある（有(あ)る・在(あ)る） have・exist　たぶん（多分(たぶん)） probably
きのう（昨日(きのう)） yesterday

**4)** Numbers are usually shown as Arabic numerals:

e.g. 9時(じ) nine o'clock　4月1日(がつついたち) 1st April　1つ(ひと) one

## Ⅵ. Miscellaneous

**1)** Words that can be omitted are enclosed in square brackets:

e.g. 父(ちち)は 54［歳(さい)］です。 My father is 54 [years old].

**2)** Synonymous words and expressions are enclosed in round brackets:

e.g. だれ（どなた） who

# HOW TO USE THIS BOOK EFFECTIVELY

### 1. Learn the words

The Translation and Grammar Notes introduces the new words for each lesson. Learn these new words by practising making short sentences with them.

### 2. Practise the Sentence Patterns

Make sure you understand the meaning of each sentence pattern, and do Exercises A and B aloud until the pattern becomes automatic.

### 3. Practise holding conversations

Practise the sentence patterns using the short dialogues given in Exercise C, but don't stop there; carry on and extend the conversations. The conversations simulate everyday situations that students are likely to encounter, and the best way of acquiring a natural conversational rhythm is to act out the conversations using gestures and facial expressions while listening to the CD.

### 4. Check your understanding

Each lesson ends with some practice questions which you should use to check that you have correctly understood the lesson.

### 5. Apply what you have learnt

Try talking to Japanese people using the Japanese you have learnt. Applying what you have learnt right away, before you forget it, is the quickest way to progress.

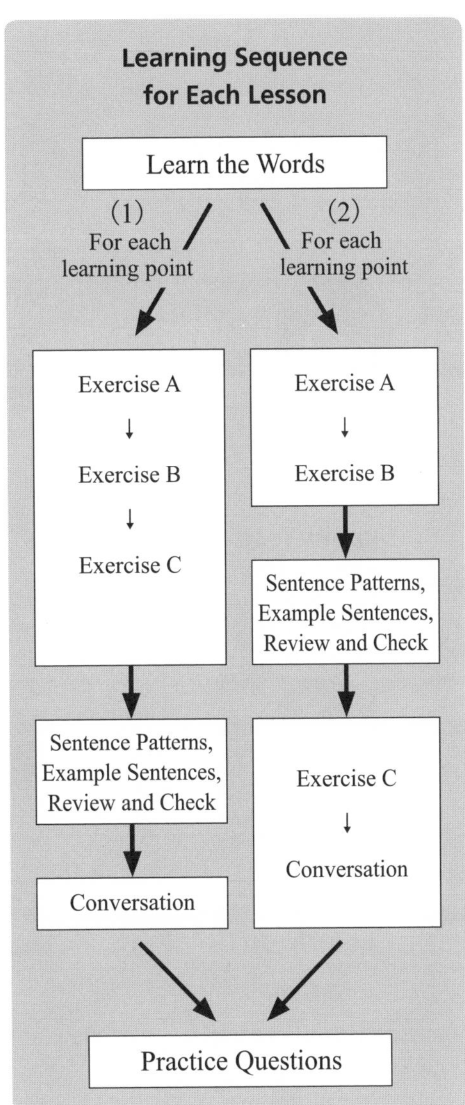


Study the material by following either Route (1) or Route (2). To make sure you cover all the key learning points, please check the Table of Key Learning Points at the end of this book.

# CHARACTERS

**Mike Miller**
American,
employee of IMC

**Suzuki Yasuo**
Japanese,
employee of IMC

**Nakamura Akiko**
Japanese,
Sales Section Manager at IMC

**Lee Jin Ju**
Korean,
research worker at AKC

**Thawaphon**
Thai,
student at Sakura University

**Karina**
Indonesian,
student at Fuji University

**Ogawa Hiroshi**
Japanese,
neighbour of Mike Miller's

**Ogawa Yone**
Japanese,
Ogawa Hiroshi's mother

**Ogawa Sachiko**
Japanese,
company employee

**Karl Schmidt**

German,
engineer at Power Electric Company

**Klara Schmidt**

German,
teacher of German

**Ito Chiseko**

Japanese,
Hans Schmidt's class teacher at
Himawari Elementary School

**Watanabe Akemi**

Japanese, employee of Power
Electric Company

**Takahashi Toru**

Japanese, employee of Power
Electric Company

**Hayashi Makiko**

Japanese, employee of Power
Electric Company

**John Watt**

British,
English teacher at Sakura University

**Matsumoto Tadashi**

Japanese,
Department Manager at IMC (Osaka)

**Matsumoto Yoshiko**

Japanese, housewife

**Hans**

German,
12-year-old schoolboy,
son of Karl and Klara Schmidt

**Gupta**

Indian,
employee of IMC

**Kimura Izumi**

Japanese, announcer

※IMC（computer software company）

※AKC（アジア研究(けんきゅう)センター：Asia Research Institute）

# CONTENTS

# GRAMMAR NOTES, AND USEFUL WORDS AND INFORMATION IN みんなの日本語　初級Ⅰ　第2版

## Lesson 1

1. $N_1$は $N_2$です
2. $N_1$は $N_2$じゃ(では) ありません
3. $N_1$は $N_2$ですか
4. Nも
5. $N_1$の $N_2$
6. ～さん

U & I　**Countries, People and Languages**

## Lesson 2

1. これ／それ／あれ
2. この N／その N／あの N
3. そうです
4. ～か、～か
5. $N_1$の $N_2$
6. の substituting for a noun
7. お～
8. そうですか

U & I　**Family Names**

## Lesson 3

1. ここ／そこ／あそこ／こちら／そちら／あちら
2. Nは placeです
3. どこ／どちら
4. $N_1$の $N_2$
5. The こ／そ／あ／ど system of demonstratives
6. お～

U & I　**Department Store**

## Lesson 4

1. 今 －時－分です
2. Vます／Vません／Vました／Vませんでした
3. N (time)に V
4. $N_1$から $N_2$まで
5. $N_1$と $N_2$
6. ～ね

U & I　**Telephone and Letters**

## Lesson 5

1. N (place)へ 行きます／来ます／帰ります
2. どこ[へ]も 行きません／行きませんでした
3. N (vehicle)で 行きます／来ます／帰ります
4. N (person/animal)と V
5. いつ
6. ～よ
7. そうですね

U & I　**National Holidays**

## Lesson 6

1. Nを V (transitive)
2. Nを します
3. 何を しますか
4. なん and なに
5. N (place)で V
6. Vませんか
7. Vましょう
8. ～か

U & I　**Food**

## Lesson 7

1. N (tool/means) で V
2. 'Word/Sentence' は ～語(ご)で 何(なん)ですか
3. $N_1$ (person) に $N_2$ を あげます, etc.
4. $N_1$ (person) に $N_2$ を もらいます, etc.
5. もう Vました
6. Omission of particles

U & I **Family**

## Lesson 8

1. Adjectives
2. Nは な-adj [な] です
   Nは い-adj (～い) です
3. な-adj な N
   い-adj (～い) N
4. ～が、～
5. とても／あまり
6. Nは どうですか
7. $N_1$は どんな $N_2$ですか
8. そうですね

U & I **Colours and Tastes**

## Lesson 9

1. Nが あります／わかります
   Nが 好(す)きです／嫌(きら)いです／
   上手(じょうず)です／下手(へた)です
2. どんな N
3. よく／だいたい／たくさん／少(すこ)し／
   あまり／全然(ぜんぜん)
4. ～から、～
5. どうして

U & I **Music, Sports and Films**

## Lesson 10

1. Nが あります／います
2. Placeに Nが あります／います
3. Nは placeに あります／います
4. $N_1$ (thing/person/place) の $N_2$ (position)
5. $N_1$ や $N_2$
6. アジアストアですか

U & I **Inside the House**

## Lesson 11

1. How to say numbers
2. How to use quantifiers
3. Quantifier (time period) に －回(かい) V
4. Quantifier だけ／N だけ

U & I **Menu**

## Lesson 12

1. Tense and affirmative/negative forms of noun sentences and な-adjective sentences
2. Tense and affirmative/negative forms of い-adjective sentences
3. $N_1$は $N_2$より adj です
4. $N_1$と $N_2$と どちらが adj ですか
   ……$N_1$ ／ $N_2$の ほうが adj です
5. $N_1$ [の 中(なか)] で 何(なに)／どこ／だれ／いつ が いちばん adj ですか
   ……$N_2$が いちばん adj です
6. Adj の (の substituting for a noun)

U & I **Festivals and Places of Note**

## Lesson 13

1. Nが 欲(ほ)しいです
2. Vます-formたいです
3. N (place)へ {Vます-form / N} に 行(い)きます／来(き)ます／帰(かえ)ります
4. どこか／何(なに)か
5. ご～

**U & I Town**

## Lesson 14

1. Verb Groups
2. Vて-form
3. Vて-form ください
4. Vて-form います
5. Vます-formましょうか
6. Nが V
7. すみませんが

**U & I Station**

## Lesson 15

1. Vて-formも いいですか
2. Vて-formは いけません
3. Vて-form います
4. Nに V
5. $N_1$に $N_2$を V

**U & I Occupations**

## Lesson 16

1. How to join two or more sentences together
2. $V_1$て-formから、$V_2$
3. $N_1$は $N_2$が adj
4. Nを V
5. どうやって
6. どれ／どの N

**U & I How to Use a Cash Machine**

## Lesson 17

1. Vない-form
2. Vない-formないで ください
3. Vない-formなければ なりません
4. Vない-formなくても いいです
5. Making an object the topic of a sentence
6. N (time)までに V

**U & I Body and Illness**

## Lesson 18

1. Dictionary form of verbs
2. {N / V-dictionary form こと} が できます
3. わたしの 趣味(しゅみ)は {N / V-dictionary form こと} です
4. {$V_1$-dictionary form / Nの / Quantifier (time period)} まえに、$V_2$
5. なかなか
6. ぜひ

**U & I Actions**

## Lesson 19

1. Vた-form
2. Vた-form ことが あります
3. $V_1$た-formり、$V_2$た-formり します
4. い-adj (〜~~い~~)→〜く / な-adj [~~な~~]→〜に / Nに } なります

**U & I　Traditional Culture and Entertainment**

## Lesson 20

1. Polite style and plain style
2. Proper use of the polite style or plain style
3. Conversation in the plain style

**U & I　How to Address People**

## Lesson 21

1. Plain form と 思(おも)います
2. "Sentences" / Plain form } と 言(い)います
3. V / い-adj } plain form; な-adj / N } plain form 〜~~だ~~ } でしょう？
4. $N_1$ (place) で $N_2$が あります
5. N (occasion) で
6. Nでも V
7. Vない-formないと……

**U & I　Positions in Society**

## Lesson 22

1. Noun modification
2. V-dictionary form 時間(じかん)／約束(やくそく)／用事(ようじ)
3. Vます-formましょうか

**U & I　Clothes**

## Lesson 23

1. V-dictionary form / Vない-formない / い-adj (〜い) / な-adj な / Nの } とき、〜(main clause)
2. V-dictionary form / Vた-form } とき、〜(main clause)
3. V-dictionary formと、〜 (main clause)
4. Nが adj
5. Nを motionV

**U & I　Roads and Traffic**

## Lesson 24

1. くれます
2. Vて-form { あげます / もらいます / くれます
3. $N_1$は $N_2$が V

**U & I　Exchanging Gifts**

## Lesson 25

1. Plain past formら、〜 (main clause)
2. Vた-formら、〜 (main clause)
3. Vて-form / Vない-formなくて / い-adj (〜~~い~~)→〜くて / な-adj [~~な~~]→〜で / Nで } も、〜(main clause)
4. もし
5. Subject of a subordinate clause

**U & I　Life**

# TERMS USED FOR INSTRUCTION

| | | |
|---|---|---|
| 第一課 | だい　か | Lesson - |
| 文型 | ぶんけい | Sentence Pattern |
| 例文 | れいぶん | Example Sentence |
| 会話 | かいわ | Conversation |
| 練習 | れんしゅう | Exercise |
| 問題 | もんだい | Practice Question |
| 答え | こた | Answer |
| 読み物 | よ　もの | Text |
| 復習 | ふくしゅう | Review |
| | | |
| 目次 | もくじ | Contents |
| | | |
| 索引 | さくいん | Index |
| | | |
| 文法 | ぶんぽう | grammar |
| 文 | ぶん | sentence |
| | | |
| 単語(語) | たんご　ご | word |
| 句 | く | phrase |
| 節 | せつ | clause |
| | | |
| 発音 | はつおん | pronunciation |
| 母音 | ぼいん | vowel |
| 子音 | しいん | consonant |
| 拍 | はく | mora |
| アクセント | | accent |
| イントネーション | | intonation |
| | | |
| [か]行 | ぎょう | [か]row |
| [い]列 | れつ | [い]column |
| | | |
| 丁寧体 | ていねいたい | polite style of speech |
| 普通体 | ふつうたい | plain style of speech |
| 活用 | かつよう | inflection, conjugation |
| フォーム | | form |
| ～形 | けい | ～ form |
| 修飾 | しゅうしょく | modification |
| 例外 | れいがい | exception |

| | | |
|---|---|---|
| 名詞 | めいし | noun |
| 動詞 | どうし | verb |
| 　自動詞 | じどうし | intransitive verb |
| 　他動詞 | たどうし | transitive verb |
| 形容詞 | けいようし | adjective |
| 　い形容詞 | けいようし | い-adjective |
| 　な形容詞 | けいようし | な-adjective |
| 助詞 | じょし | particle |
| 副詞 | ふくし | adverb |
| 接続詞 | せつぞくし | conjunction |
| 数詞 | すうし | numeral |
| 助数詞 | じょすうし | counter suffix |
| 疑問詞 | ぎもんし | interrogative |
| | | |
| 名詞文 | めいしぶん | noun (predicate) sentence |
| 動詞文 | どうしぶん | verb (predicate) sentence |
| 形容詞文 | けいようしぶん | adjective (predicate) sentence |
| | | |
| 主語 | しゅご | subject |
| 述語 | じゅつご | predicate |
| 目的語 | もくてきご | object |
| 主題 | しゅだい | topic |
| | | |
| 肯定 | こうてい | affirmative |
| 否定 | ひてい | negative |
| 完了 | かんりょう | perfective |
| 未完了 | みかんりょう | imperfective |
| 過去 | かこ | past |
| 非過去 | ひかこ | non-past |
| | | |
| 可能 | かのう | potential |
| 意向 | いこう | volitional |
| 命令 | めいれい | imperative |
| 禁止 | きんし | prohibitive |
| 条件 | じょうけん | conditional |
| 受身 | うけみ | passive |
| 使役 | しえき | causative |
| 尊敬 | そんけい | respectful |
| 謙譲 | けんじょう | humble |

# KEY TO SYMBOLS AND ABBREVIATIONS

## 1. Symbols Used in I. Vocabulary

① ～ indicates a missing word or phrase

e.g. ～から 来ました。 came from ～

② － indicates a missing number

e.g. －歳 － years old

③ Words and phrases that can be omitted are enclosed in square brackets:

e.g. どうぞ よろしく [お願いします]。 Pleased to meet you.

④ Synonymous words and phrases are enclosed in round brackets:

e.g. だれ(どなた) who

⑤ Words marked with a star (＊) are not used in that lesson but are presented as being relevant.

⑥ The Conversation section (**〈会話〉**) presents words and expressions used in the lesson's Conversation.

⑦ Words and phrases appearing in the reading passages are presented in **〈読み物〉**.

⑧ ※ indicates a proper noun.



## 2. Abbreviations Used in IV. Grammar Notes

| | | |
|---|---|---|
| N | noun (名詞) | e.g. がくせい(student) つくえ(desk) |
| い-adj | い-adjective (い形容詞) | e.g. おいしい(delicious)<br>たかい(high, expensive) |
| な-adj | な-adjective (な形容詞) | e.g. きれい[な](beautiful)<br>しずか[な](quiet) |
| V | verb (動詞) | e.g. かきます(write) たべます(eat) |
| S | sentence (文) | e.g. これは 本です。 This is a book.<br>わたしは あした 東京へ 行きます。<br>I'm going to Tokyo tomorrow. |

# Lesson 26

## I. Vocabulary

| | | |
|---|---|---|
| みますⅡ | 見ます、診ます | check, take a look at |
| さがしますⅠ | 探します、捜します | look for, search |
| おくれますⅡ<br>［じかんに～］ | 遅れます<br>［時間に～］ | be late [for an appointment, etc.] |
| まに あいますⅠ<br>［じかんに～］ | 間に 合います<br>［時間に～］ | be in time [for an appointment, etc.] |
| やりますⅠ | | do |
| ひろいますⅠ | 拾います | pick up |
| れんらくしますⅢ | 連絡します | contact, get in touch with |
| きぶんが いい* | 気分が いい | feel well |
| きぶんが わるい | 気分が 悪い | feel ill |
| うんどうかい | 運動会 | athletic meeting, sports day |
| ぼんおどり | 盆踊り | Bon Festival dance |
| フリーマーケット | | flea market |
| ばしょ | 場所 | place |
| ボランティア | | volunteer |
| さいふ | 財布 | wallet, purse |
| ごみ | | garbage, rubbish, dust |
| こっかいぎじどう | 国会議事堂 | the Diet Building |
| へいじつ | 平日 | weekday |
| ～べん | ～弁 | ～ dialect |
| こんど | 今度 | next time, another time |
| ずいぶん | | very, pretty |
| ちょくせつ | 直接 | directly |
| いつでも | | any time |
| どこでも* | | anywhere |
| だれでも* | | anybody |
| なんでも* | 何でも | anything |
| こんな ～* | | ～ like this |
| そんな ～ | | ～ like that (near the listener) |
| あんな ～* | | ～ like that (far from both the speaker and the listener) |
| ※エドヤストア | | fictitious store |

### 〈会話（かいわ）〉

| | |
|---|---|
| 片（かた）づきます I ［荷物（にもつ）が～］ | [boxes] be put in order, tidy up |
| 出（だ）します I ［ごみを～］ | put out [the rubbish] |
| 燃（も）える ごみ | burnable rubbish |
| 置（お）き場（ば） | place where something is put |
| 横（よこ） | side |
| 瓶（びん） | bottle |
| 缶（かん） | can |
| ガス | gas |
| ～会社（がいしゃ） | ～ company |

### 〈読（よ）み物（もの）〉

| | |
|---|---|
| 宇宙（うちゅう） | space, universe |
| ～様（さま） | Mr. ～/Ms. ～（respectful equivalent of～さん） |
| 宇宙船（うちゅうせん） | spaceship |
| 怖（こわ）い | be afraid of |
| 宇宙（うちゅう）ステーション | space station |
| 違（ちが）います I | be different |
| 宇宙飛行士（うちゅうひこうし） | astronaut |
| ※星出彰彦（ほしであきひこ） | Japanese astronaut（1968- ） |

## II. Translation

### Sentence Patterns

1. I'm going away on holiday tomorrow.
2. I'd like to study flower arranging; could you introduce me to a good teacher?

### Example Sentences

1. You occasionally speak in the Osaka dialect, don't you, Ms. Watanabe?
   Have you lived in Osaka?
   ······Yes, I lived in Osaka until I was fifteen.
2. Those shoes are interestingly designed, aren't they? Where did you buy them?
   ······I bought them at Edoya Store. They're Spanish.
3. Why were you late?
   ······Because the bus didn't come.
4. Do you often go to karaoke?
   ······No, I don't go very often; I don't like karaoke.
5. I've written a report in Japanese. Would you mind taking a quick look at it?
   ······No problem.
6. I'd like to visit the National Diet. How should I go about it?
   ······You can go right there. It's always open on weekdays.



### Conversation

**Where should I put the rubbish?**

Caretaker: Hello, Mr. Miller. Have you sorted out the things you brought with you when you moved in?
Miller: Yes, I've more or less tidied up.
By the way, I want to put my rubbish out. Where should I put it?
Caretaker: Please put burnable rubbish out on Monday and Thursday mornings.
The rubbish collection point is beside the car park.
Miller: When should bottles and cans go out?
Caretaker: On Saturdays.
Miller: I see. And I haven't got any hot water......
Caretaker: If you contact the gas company, they'll come right away.
Miller: Would you mind giving me their telephone number?
Caretaker: No problem.

## III. Useful Words & Information

### ごみの出(だ)し方(かた)　Refuse Disposal

In order to reduce and recycle refuse, household waste is sorted into types and collected on different days. The designated collection sites and collection days vary from area to area. The following is an example of the regulations.

ごみ収集(しゅうしゅう)日(び)のお知(し)らせ

Refuse Collection Day Information

可燃(かねん)ごみ（燃(も)えるごみ）
Burnable Refuse

生(なま)ごみ、紙(かみ)くずなど
Kitchen waste, paper, etc.

収集日(しゅうしゅうび)：月曜日(げつようび)・木曜日(もくようび)
Collection days: Monday and Thursday

不燃(ふねん)ごみ（燃(も)えないごみ）
Non-Burnable Refuse

ガラス製品(せいひん)、瀬戸物(せともの)、金属製台所用品(きんぞくせいだいどころようひん)など
Glass, china, metal kitchen utensils, etc.

収集日(しゅうしゅうび)：水曜日(すいようび)
Collection day: Wednesday

資源(しげん)ごみ
Recyclable Refuse

缶(かん)、瓶(びん)、ペットボトルなど
Cans, glass bottles, plastic bottles, etc.

収集日(しゅうしゅうび)：第(だい)２、第(だい)４火曜日(かようび)
Collection days: Second and fourth Tuesdays

粗大(そだい)ごみ
Bulky Refuse

家具(かぐ)、自転車(じてんしゃ)など
Furniture, bicycles, etc.

事前申(じぜんもう)し込(こ)み
Call in advance

## IV. Grammar Notes

**1.**

| | | | |
|---|---|---|---|
| V<br>い -adj | plain form | | んです |
| な -adj<br>N | plain form<br>～だ→～な | | |

～んです is used in speech. In writing, ～のです is used.

～んです is used in the following ways:

1）～んですか

（1）When asking the listener to confirm something that the speaker has seen or heard:

① （ぬれた 傘(かさ)を 持(も)って いる 人(ひと)を 見(み)て） 雨(あめ)が 降(ふ)って いるんですか。

(On seeing someone holding a wet umbrella) Is it raining?

（2）When asking the listener for more detailed information about something that the speaker has seen or heard:

② おもしろい デザインの 靴(くつ)ですね。どこで 買(か)ったんですか。

Those shoes are interestingly designed, aren't they? Where did you buy them?

（3）When asking the listener for a reason for something that the speaker has seen or heard:

③ どうして 遅(おく)れたんですか。　　Why were you late?

（4）When asking for an explanation of a situation:

④ どう したんですか。　　What's the matter?



[Note] Be careful not to use ～んですか when it is not needed, as this will sound strange to the listener.

2）～んです

（1）When giving a reason or explanation in reply to a sentence with ～んですか in it such as those in（3）or（4）in 1）above:

⑤ どうして 遅(おく)れたんですか。　　Why were you late?

……バスが 来(こ)なかったんです。　　…… Because the bus didn't come.

⑥ どう したんですか。

……ちょっと 気分(きぶん)が 悪(わる)いんです。

What's the matter?

…… I don't feel very well.

（2）When adding a reason to explain something one has just said:

⑦ よく カラオケに 行(い)きますか。

……いいえ、あまり 行(い)きません。カラオケは 好(す)きじゃ ないんです。

Do you often go to karaoke?

…… No, I don't go very often. I don't like karaoke.

[Note] ～んです is not used when not giving a reason but merely stating a fact:

×わたしは マイク・ミラーなんです。

3) ～んですが、～

～んですが is used to introduce a topic when this is followed by a request, an invitation, or an expression seeking permission. The が in this case is used to lightly preface what is coming next (see Lesson 14). What follows ～んですが may be omitted when it is obvious, as in example ⑩:

⑧ 頭が 痛いんですが、帰っても いいですか。

I've got a headache; may I go home?

⑨ 来週 友達と スキーに 行くんですが、ミラーさんも いっしょに 行きませんか。

I'm going skiing with some friends next week. Would you like to come too, Mr. Miller?

⑩ お湯が 出ないんですが……。　There's no hot water......

## 2. V て -form いただけませんか　Would you be so kind as to ～?

This is a more polite way of asking for something than ～て ください:

⑪ いい 先生を 紹介して いただけませんか。

Would you be so kind as to introduce me to a good teacher?

## 3. Interrogative V た -form ら いいですか　What/When/Where/Which/How/Who should I ～?

This is a way of asking for advice or instructions:

⑫ どこで カメラを 買ったら いいですか。

……ABC ストアが 安いですよ。

Where would be a good place to buy a camera?

…… ABC Store is cheap, you know.

⑬ 国会議事堂を 見学したいんですが、どう したら いいですか。

……直接 行ったら いいですよ。

I'd like to visit the National Diet; how should I go about it?

…… You can go right there, you know.

As illustrated in Example ⑬, the expression V た -form ら いいですよ can be used to advise someone about something or recommend something to them.

## 4. N (object) は { 好きです／嫌いです / 上手です／下手です / あります, etc. }　{ like/dislike / be good at/be no good at / have, etc. } N

⑭ よく カラオケに 行きますか。

……いいえ、あまり 行きません。カラオケは 好きじゃ ないんです。

Do you often go to karaoke?

…… No, I don't go very often. I don't like karaoke.

Making a direct object marked by を into the topic of a sentence was introduced in Lesson 17 of Book I. Nouns indicated by が that are the object of phrases such as すきです can also be made into a topic, as in Example ⑭.

# Lesson 27

## I. Vocabulary

| | | |
|---|---|---|
| かいますⅠ | 飼います | keep (a pet), raise (an animal) |
| はしりますⅠ [みちを～] | 走ります [道を～] | run, drive [along a road] |
| みえますⅡ [やまが～] | 見えます [山が～] | [a mountain] can be seen |
| きこえますⅡ [おとが～] | 聞こえます [音が～] | [a sound] can be heard |
| できますⅡ [みちが～] | [道が～] | [a road] be made, be completed, come into existence |
| ひらきますⅠ [きょうしつを～] | 開きます [教室を～] | set up [a class], open, hold |
| しんぱい[な] | 心配[な] | worried, anxious |
| ペット | | pet |
| とり | 鳥 | bird |
| こえ | 声 | voice |
| なみ | 波 | wave |
| はなび | 花火 | fireworks |
| どうぐ | 道具 | tool, instrument, equipment |
| クリーニング | | (dry) cleaning, laundry |
| いえ | 家 | house, home |
| マンション | | condominium, apartment house, blocks of flats |
| キッチン | | kitchen |
| ～きょうしつ | ～教室 | ～ class |
| パーティールーム | | party room |
| かた | 方 | person (respectful equivalent of ひと) |
| ～ご | ～後 | after ～ (duration of time) |
| ～しか | | only ～ (used with negatives) |
| ほかの | | other |
| はっきり | | clearly |

**〈会話（かいわ）〉**

| | |
|---|---|
| 家具（かぐ） | furniture |
| 本棚（ほんだな） | bookcase |
| いつか | one day, some day |
| 建（た）てますⅡ | build |
| すばらしい | wonderful |

**〈読（よ）み物（もの）〉**

| | |
|---|---|
| 子（こ）どもたち | children |
| 大好（だいす）き［な］ | like very much |
| 主人公（しゅじんこう） | hero, heroine |
| 形（かたち） | shape |
| 不思議（ふしぎ）［な］ | fantastic, mysterious |
| ポケット | pocket |
| 例（たと）えば | for example |
| 付（つ）けますⅡ | attach, put on |
| 自由（じゆう）に | freely |
| 空（そら） | sky |
| 飛（と）びますⅠ | fly |
| 昔（むかし） | old days, ancient times |
| 自分（じぶん） | oneself |
| 将来（しょうらい） | future |
| | |
| ※ドラえもん | name of a cartoon character |

## II. Translation

### Sentence Patterns



1. I can speak a little Japanese.
2. The mountains are clearly visible.
3. A large supermarket has been built in front of the station.

### Example Sentences

1. Can you read Japanese newspapers?
   ······No, I can't.
2. You can hear birds singing, can't you?
   ······Yes, it's already spring, isn't it?
3. When was Horyuji built?
   ······In 607.
4. How many days' summer holiday do you get at Power Electric?
   ······Hmm... About three weeks.
   That's good, isn't it? At my company, we only get one week.
5. Can you keep pets in this block of flats?
   ······We can keep small birds or fish, but not dogs or cats.



### Conversation

**You can make anything, can't you?**

Miller: This is a nice bright room, isn't it?
Suzuki: Yes. On a fine day, you can see the sea.
Miller: This table has an interesting design, doesn't it?
Where did you buy it?
Suzuki: I made it myself.
Miller: Oh, really?
Suzuki: Yes. My hobby is furniture-making.
Miller: Oh. So did you make that bookcase as well?
Suzuki: Yes.
Miller: That's amazing. You can make anything, can't you, Mr. Suzuki?
Suzuki: My dream is to build my own house one day.
Miller: What a wonderful dream!

## III. Useful Words & Information

### 近くの店　Local Shops

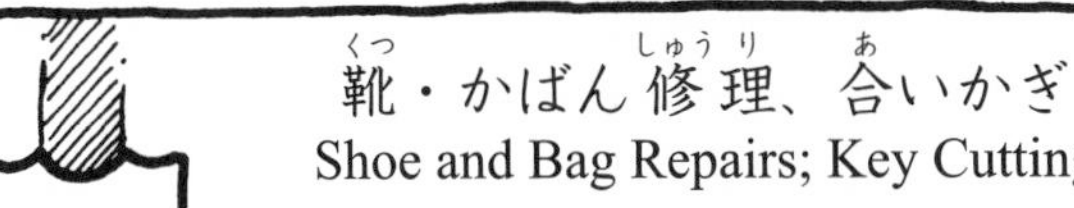

#### 靴・かばん修理、合いかぎ
Shoe and Bag Repairs; Key Cutting

| | |
|---|---|
| ヒール・かかと修理 | Heels replaced |
| つま先修理 | Toes repaired and reinforced |
| 中敷き交換 | Inserts changed |
| クリーニング | Dry cleaning |
| ファスナー交換 | Fasteners replaced |
| ハンドル・持ち手交換 | Handles and grips replaced |
| ほつれ・縫い目の修理 | Frayed items and seams repaired |
| 合いかぎ | Keys cut |

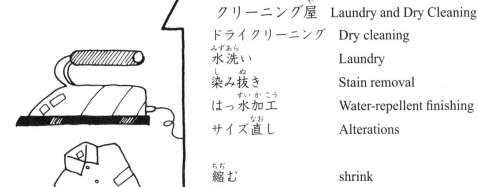

#### クリーニング屋　Laundry and Dry Cleaning

| | |
|---|---|
| ドライクリーニング | Dry cleaning |
| 水洗い | Laundry |
| 染み抜き | Stain removal |
| はっ水加工 | Water-repellent finishing |
| サイズ直し | Alterations |
| 縮む | shrink |
| 伸びる | stretch |

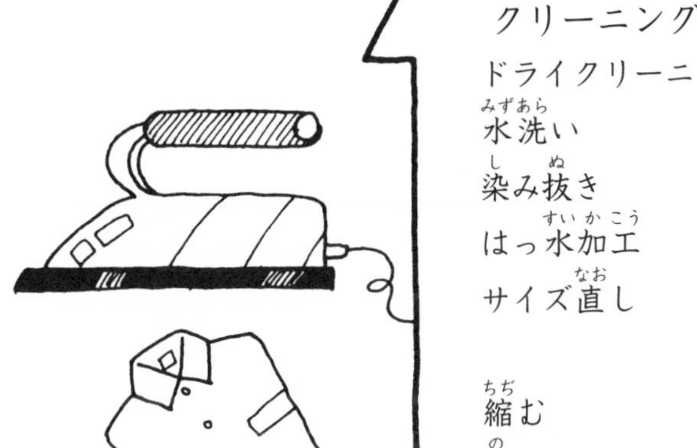



#### コンビニ　Convenience Store

| | |
|---|---|
| 宅配便の受け付け | Home delivery service |
| ATM | Cash machine, ATM (Automatic Teller Machine) |
| 公共料金等の支払い | Payment of public utility charges, etc. |
| コピー、ファクス | Photocopying, faxing |
| はがき・切手の販売 | Sale of postcards and stamps |
| コンサートチケットの販売 | Sale of concert tickets |

## IV. Grammar Notes

### 1. Potential verbs

N／V dictionary-form ＋ことが できます was explained in Lesson 18 of Book I as a form expressing potential. This lesson explains potential verbs in another form.

| | | Potential verbs | |
|---|---|---|---|
| | | Polite form | Plain form |
| I | かきます<br>かいます | かけます<br>かえます | かける<br>かえる |
| II | たべます | たべられます | たべられる |
| III | きます<br>します | こられます<br>できます | こられる<br>できる |

(See Exercise A1, Lesson 27, Main Text)

Potential verbs are conjugated as Group II verbs.

Examples: かえます　　かえる　　かえ(ない)　　かえて

Note that because わかります already includes the meaning of possibility, it does not take the form わかれます.

### 2. Sentences in which potential verbs are used

1) Potential verbs indicate states, not actions. Thus, although the object of a transitive verb is indicated by the particle を, the object of a potential verb is usually indicated by が:

① わたしは 日本語(にほんご)を 話(はな)します。　I speak Japanese.

② わたしは 日本語(にほんご)が 話(はな)せます。　I can speak Japanese.

Particles other than を remain the same:

③ 一人(ひとり)で 病院(びょういん)へ 行(い)けますか。　Can you get to the hospital on your own?

④ 田中(たなか)さんに 会(あ)えませんでした。　I was unable to meet Mr. Tanaka.

2) A potential verb can be used to state someone's ability to do something, as in example ⑤, or to indicate that an action is possible in a certain situation, as in example ⑥:

⑤ ミラーさんは 漢字(かんじ)が 読(よ)めます。 Mr. Miller can read kanji.

⑥ この 銀行(ぎんこう)で ドルが 換(か)えられます。

You can change dollars at this bank.

### 3. 見(み)えます and 聞(き)こえます

みえます and きこえます are not volitional; they denote something (indicated by が) naturally coming into sight, or a sound naturally reaching one's ears, independent of one's will. みえます and きこえます cannot be used to talk about a person deliberately paying attention to something; in that case, a potential verb is used:

⑦ 新幹線(しんかんせん)から 富士山(ふじさん)が 見(み)えます。

You can see Mount Fuji from the Shinkansen.

⑧ ラジオの 音(おと)が 聞(き)こえます。

The sound of a radio can be heard.

⑨ 新宿で 今 黒沢の 映画が 見られます。

You can watch a Kurosawa film in Shinjuku at the moment.

⑩ 電話で 天気予報が 聞けます。

You can listen to the weather forecast on the telephone.

## 4. できます

The sense of the verb できます introduced here is to 'come into being', 'be completed', 'be finished', 'be made', etc:

⑪ 駅の 前に 大きい スーパーが できました。

A big supermarket was built in front of the station.

⑫ 時計の 修理は いつ できますか。

When can you repair this watch by?

## 5. しか

しか is appended to nouns, quantifiers, etc., and is always used with a negative. A sentence that contains it negates everything except the word to which it is attached. When used with a noun to which a particle is attached, it is appended to the particle unless this is が or を, which it replaces. It suggests insufficiency or inadequacy:

⑬ ローマ字しか 書けません。　　I can only write Romaji.

⑭ ローマ字だけ 書けます。　　I can write Romaji [but nothing else].

## 6. N は (contrast)

In addition to introducing a topic, は can also indicate a contrast:

⑮ ワインは 飲みますが、ビールは 飲みません。

I drink wine, but I don't drink beer.

⑯ きのうは 山が 見えましたが、きょうは 見えません。

The mountains were visible yesterday, but not today.

## 7. は used to highlight a word with another particle already attached

As explained in Book I Article 1 (p.160), when は is used with a noun to which another particle is already attached, it is appended to the particle unless the particle is が or を, which it replaces:

⑰ 日本では 馬を 見る ことが できません。

You can't see any horses in Japan. (See Lesson 18)

⑱ 天気の いい 日には 海が 見えるんです。

On a fine day, you can see the sea.

⑲ ここからは 東京スカイツリーが 見えません。

You can't see Tokyo Sky Tree from here.

# Lesson 28

## I. Vocabulary

| | | |
|---|---|---|
| うれますⅡ<br>［パンが～］ | 売れます | [bread] sell, be sold |
| おどりますⅠ | 踊ります | dance |
| かみますⅠ | | chew, bite |
| えらびますⅠ | 選びます | choose |
| かよいますⅠ<br>［だいがくに～］ | 通います<br>［大学に～］ | go to and from [university] |
| メモしますⅢ | | take a memo |
| | | |
| まじめ［な］ | | serious |
| ねっしん［な］ | 熱心［な］ | earnest |
| | | |
| えらい | 偉い | great, admirable |
| ちょうど いい | | proper, just right |
| | | |
| けしき | 景色 | scenery, view |
| びよういん | 美容院 | hair salon |
| だいどころ | 台所 | kitchen |
| | | |
| けいけん | 経験 | experience（～が あります：be experienced, ～を します：experience） |
| ちから | 力 | power |
| にんき | 人気 | popularity（［がくせいに］ ～が あります：be popular [with students]） |
| | | |
| かたち | 形 | form, shape |
| いろ | 色 | colour |
| あじ | 味 | taste |
| ガム | | chewing gum |
| | | |
| しなもの | 品物 | goods |
| ねだん | 値段 | price |
| きゅうりょう | 給料 | salary |
| ボーナス | | bonus |
| | | |
| ゲーム | | （computer） game |
| ばんぐみ | 番組 | programme |
| ドラマ | | drama |
| かしゅ | 歌手 | singer |
| しょうせつ | 小説 | novel |
| しょうせつか | 小説家 | novelist |
| ～か | ～家 | -er, -ist, etc.（e.g. painter, novelist） |
| ～き | ～機 | ～ machine |

| | | |
|---|---|---|
| むすこ | 息子 | (my) son |
| むすこさん* | 息子さん | (someone else's) son |
| むすめ | 娘 | (my) daughter |
| むすめさん* | 娘さん | (someone else's) daughter |
| じぶん | 自分 | oneself |
| | | |
| しょうらい | 将来 | future |
| しばらく | | a little while |
| たいてい | | usually, mostly |
| | | |
| それに | | in addition |
| それで | | and so |

**〈会話（かいわ）〉**

| | |
|---|---|
| [ちょっと] お願（ねが）いが あるんですが。 | I have a [small] favour to ask. |
| 実（じつ）は | as a matter of fact |
| 会話（かいわ） | conversation |
| うーん | well, let me see, hmm... |

**〈読（よ）み物（もの）〉**

| | |
|---|---|
| お知（し）らせ | notice |
| 参加（さんか）しますⅢ | participate, join, attend |
| 日（ひ）にち | date |
| 土（ど） | Saturday |
| 体育館（たいいくかん） | gymnasium |
| 無料（むりょう） | free of charge |
| 誘（さそ）いますⅠ | invite, ask someone to join |
| イベント | event |

## II. Translation

### Sentence Patterns

1. I listen to music while eating.
2. I go jogging every morning.
3. Let's go on the underground; it's quick and cheap.

### Example Sentences

1. If I feel sleepy while driving, I chew gum.
   ……Do you? I stop the car and take a nap.
2. Do you listen to music while studying?
   ……No, I don't [listen to music while studying].
3. He's working while studying at university.
   ……Is he? Good for him!
4. What do you usually do on your days off?
   ……Well, I usually paint.
5. Professor Watt is enthusiastic, interesting and experienced.
   ……He's a good teacher, isn't he?
6. Do you often come to this sushi restaurant?
   ……Yes, the prices are cheap and the fish is fresh, so I often come here.
7. Why did you choose Fuji University?
   ……Because it's well-known and has many good lecturers, and it also has student accommodation.

### Conversation

**I'm away on business a lot, and I've got an exam coming up**

Sachiko Ogawa: Mr. Miller, I have a small favour to ask.
Miller: Yes, what is it?
Sachiko Ogawa: As a matter of fact, I'm going on a homestay visit to Australia in August.
Miller: A homestay? That's great.
Sachiko Ogawa: Yes, and I'm studying English with a friend at the moment, but......
Miller: Yes?
Sachiko Ogawa: But I'm not improving very much; I don't have a teacher, and I don't have any opportunity to speak English......
I was wondering whether you would be my conversation teacher, Mr. Miller?
Miller: Me be your teacher? Hmm... I'm rather busy with work......
Sachiko Ogawa: Only when you're free, over a cup of tea or something......
Miller: Hmm... I'm away on business a lot, and I've got my Japanese exam soon as well......
Sachiko Ogawa: Oh.
Miller: Sorry.

## III. Useful Words & Information

### うちを借りる　Renting Accommodation

Understanding Rental Information

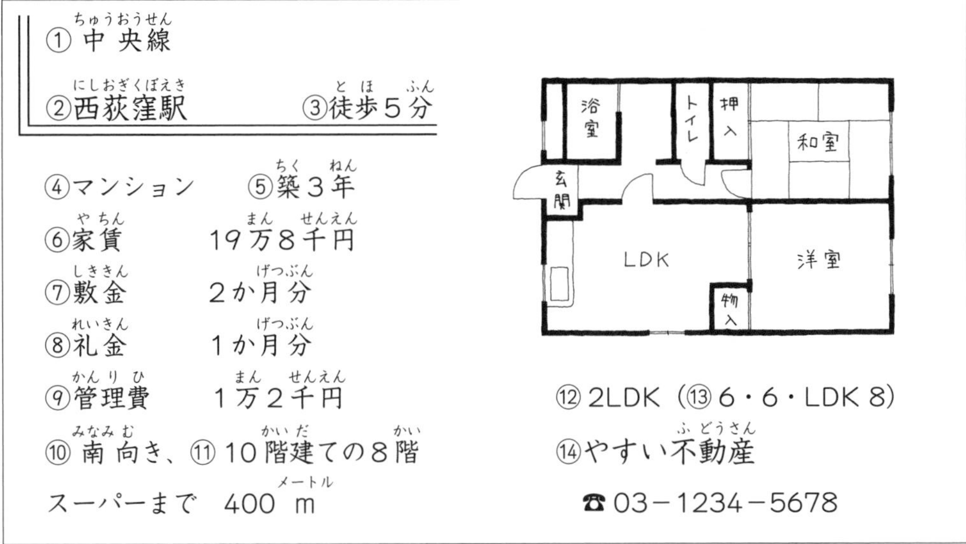

①中央線
②西荻窪駅
③徒歩5分
④マンション
⑤築3年
⑥家賃　19万8千円
⑦敷金　2か月分
⑧礼金　1か月分
⑨管理費　1万2千円
⑩南向き、⑪10階建ての8階
スーパーまで　400 m
浴室
トイレ
押入
和室
玄関
LDK
洋室
物入
⑫2LDK（⑬6・6・LDK 8）
⑭やすい不動産
☎03−1234−5678


① Name of train line
② Name of nearest station
③ five-minute walk from the station
④ condominium of reinforced concrete construction
　※アパート　one or two-storey wooden apartment building
　一戸建て　detached house
⑤ three years old (years since construction)
⑥ monthly rent
⑦ deposit
　※ Money left with the landlord as a deposit. When a tenant moves out, the landlord should return some or all of it.
⑧ key money
　※ Money paid to the landlord as a 'gift'.
⑨ monthly maintenance fee
⑩ south-facing
⑪ 8th floor of 10-storey building
⑫ 1 combined living room/dining room/kitchen, and 2 other rooms
⑬ 6 mats (= 6 畳)
　※ A '畳' is a unit of measurement for the area of a room. 1 畳 corresponds to the area of one tatami mat (approximately 180×90 cm).
⑭ name of estate agent

## IV. Grammar Notes

### 1. $V_1$ ます -form ながら $V_2$

This sentence pattern indicates that someone performing an action indicated by $V_1$ is simultaneously performing a separate action indicated by $V_2$, where $V_2$ indicates the main action:

① 音楽を 聞きながら 食事します。

I listen to music while eating.

It is also used to describe someone doing two things continuously over a period of time:

② 働きながら 日本語を 勉強して います。

I'm working while studying Japanese.

### 2. V て -form います

As well as indicating what someone is doing now, this sentence pattern can also be used to indicate a habitual behaviour. Such a behaviour taking place in the past is indicated by V て -form いました:

③ 毎朝 ジョギングを して います。

I go jogging every morning.

④ 子どもの とき、毎晩 8時に 寝て いました。

When I was a child, I used to go to bed at eight every evening.



### 3. Plain form し、plain form し、～

1) This sentence pattern is used when mentioning two or more similar things one after the other about the topic. In Example ⑤, the things mentioned are similar because they are all accomplishments:

⑤ 鈴木さんは ピアノも 弾けるし、歌も 歌えるし、ダンスも できます。

Mr. Suzuki can play the piano, sing, and dance.

Since this sentence pattern expresses the speaker's desire to mention more than just one thing about the topic, も is also often used. それに can also be used to make this meaning even clearer, as in example ⑥:

⑥ 田中さんは まじめだし、中国語も 上手だし、それに 経験も あります。

Mr. Tanaka is serious, speaks good Chinese, and also has experience.

2) This sentence pattern can also be used when the ～し、～し part gives the reasons for what follows:

⑦ ここは 値段も 安いし、魚も 新しいし、よく 食べに 来ます。

The prices are low here and the fish is fresh, so I often come here to eat.

In this case, the conclusion may be omitted if it is obvious, leaving only the reasons:

⑧ どうして この 店へ 来るんですか。
……ここは 値段も 安いし、魚も 新しいし……。

Why do you come to this restaurant?
…… Because the prices are cheap here, and the fish is fresh......

The final し can be replaced by から in its 'because' sense:

⑨ どうして 日本の アニメが 好きなんですか。
……話も おもしろいし、音楽も すてきですから。
Why do you like Japanese anime?
…… Because the stories are interesting and I like the music.

## 4. それで

それで indicates that what is about to be said follows from what has just been said:

⑩ 将来 小説家に なりたいです。それで 今は アルバイトを しながら 小説を 書いて います。
I want to be a novelist, so now I'm writing a novel and working part-time while doing so.

⑪ ここは コーヒーも おいしいし、食事も できるし……。
……それで 人気が あるんですね。
The coffee's good here, and you can also have a meal......
…… So that's why it's popular, isn't it?

## 5. ～ とき＋ particle

Since the とき explained in Lesson 23 is a noun, it can be used with a particle appended to it:

⑫ 勉強する ときは、音楽を 聞きません。
I don't listen to music when I'm studying.

⑬ 疲れた ときや 寂しい とき、よく 田舎の 青い 空を 思い出す。
When tired or lonely, I often recall the blue skies over my home town. (See Lesson 31)

# Lesson 29

## I. Vocabulary

| | | |
|---|---|---|
| あきますⅠ<br>［ドアが～］ | 開きます | [a door] open |
| しまりますⅠ<br>［ドアが～］ | 閉まります | [a door] close, shut |
| つきますⅠ<br>［でんきが～］ | <br>［電気が～］ | [a light] come on, be turned on |
| きえますⅡ*<br>［でんきが～］ | 消えます<br>［電気が～］ | [a light] go off |
| こわれますⅡ<br>［いすが～］ | 壊れます | [a chair] break |
| われますⅡ<br>［コップが～］ | 割れます | [a glass] break, smash |
| おれますⅡ<br>［きが～］ | 折れます<br>［木が～］ | [a tree] break, snap |
| やぶれますⅡ<br>［かみが～］ | 破れます<br>［紙が～］ | [paper] tear |
| よごれますⅡ<br>［ふくが～］ | 汚れます<br>［服が～］ | [clothes] get dirty |
| つきますⅠ<br>［ポケットが～］ | 付きます | [a pocket] be attached |
| はずれますⅡ<br>［ボタンが～］ | 外れます | [a button] be undone |
| とまりますⅠ<br>［くるまが～］ | 止まります<br>［車が～］ | [a car] stop, park |
| まちがえますⅡ | | make a mistake |
| おとしますⅠ | 落とします | drop, lose |
| かかりますⅠ<br>［かぎが～］ | 掛かります | be locked |
| ふきますⅠ | | wipe |
| とりかえますⅡ | 取り替えます | change |
| かたづけますⅡ | 片づけます | put（things）in order, tidy up |
| | | |
| ［お］さら | ［お］皿 | plate, dish |
| ［お］ちゃわん* | | （rice）bowl |
| コップ | | glass（vessel） |
| ガラス | | glass（material） |
| ふくろ | 袋 | bag |
| しょるい | 書類 | document, papers |
| えだ | 枝 | branch, twig |
| | | |
| えきいん | 駅員 | station attendant |
| こうばん | 交番 | police box |
| | | |
| スピーチ | | speech（～を します：give/make a speech） |

| | | |
|---|---|---|
| へんじ | 返事 | reply, answer (～を します: reply, answer) |
| おさきに どうぞ。 | お先に どうぞ。 | After you./Go ahead, please. |
| ※源氏物語（げんじものがたり） | | 'The Tale of Genji' (a novel written by Murasaki Shikibu in the Heian Era) |

**〈会話（かいわ）〉**

| | | |
|---|---|---|
| 今（いま）の 電車（でんしゃ） | | the train which has just left |
| 忘（わす）れ物（もの） | | things left behind, lost property |
| このくらい | | about this (big) |
| ～側（がわ） | | ～ side |
| ポケット | | pocket |
| ～ 辺（へん） | | around ～, ～ about |
| 覚（おぼ）えて いません。 | | I don't remember. |
| 網棚（あみだな） | | overhead rack |
| 確（たし）か | | I'm pretty sure |
| [ああ、] よかった。 | | [Oh,] that's great!/Thank goodness! (used to express a feeling of relief) |
| ※新宿（しんじゅく） | | name of a station/district in Tokyo |

**〈読（よ）み物（もの）〉**

| | | |
|---|---|---|
| 地震（じしん） | | earthquake |
| 壁（かべ） | | wall |
| 針（はり） | | hands (of a clock) |
| 指（さ）しますⅠ | | point |
| 駅前（えきまえ） | | the area in front of a station |
| 倒（たお）れますⅡ | | fall down |
| 西（にし） | | west |
| ～の 方（ほう） | | direction of ～ |
| 燃（も）えますⅡ | | burn |
| レポーター | | reporter |

## II. Translation

### Sentence Patterns

1. The window's closed.
2. I left my umbrella on the train.



### Example Sentences

1. The meeting room's locked, isn't it?
   ……Then let's ask Ms. Watanabe to open it.
2. May I use this PC?
   ……That one's broken; please use the one over there.
3. Where's the wine that Mr. Schmidt brought?
   ……We drank it all.
4. Shall we go home together?
   ……Sorry, I want to finish writing this e-mail. Please go ahead.
5. Were you on time?
   ……No, I was late. I took the wrong turning.
6. What's the matter?
   ……I left my luggage in the taxi.



### Conversation

**I left something behind**

| | |
|---|---|
| Lee: | Excuse me, I left something on that train...... |
| Station Attendant: | What did you leave? |
| Lee: | A blue bag, about this big...... |
| | It's got a big pocket on the outside. |
| Station Attendant: | Where did you put it? |
| Lee: | I don't remember exactly where, but I put it on an overhead rack. |
| Station Attendant: | What was inside it? |
| Lee: | Let me see... I'm pretty sure there were some books and an umbrella in it. |
| Station Attendant: | All right, please wait a moment while I check. |
| | ………………………………………………………… |
| Station Attendant: | It's been found. |
| Lee: | Oh, that's great! |
| Station Attendant: | It's at Shinjuku station. What would you like to do? |
| Lee: | I'll go and get it right away. |
| Station Attendant: | All right, please go to the Shinjuku station office. |
| Lee: | I will. Thank you very much. |

## III. Useful Words & Information

### 状態(じょうたい)・様子(ようす)　State and Appearance

| | | | |
|---|---|---|---|
| 太(ふと)っている<br>fat | やせている<br>thin | 膨(ふく)らんでいる<br>bulging | 穴(あな)が開(あ)いている<br>have a hole |
| 曲(ま)がっている<br>bent | ゆがんでいる<br>distorted | へこんでいる<br>dented | ねじれている<br>twisted |
| 欠(か)けている<br>chipped | ひびが入(はい)っている<br>cracked | 腐(くさ)っている<br>rotten | |
| 乾(かわ)いている<br>dry | ぬれている<br>wet | 凍(こお)っている<br>frozen | |

## IV. Grammar Notes

### 1. V て -form います

Another way of using V て -form います is to show that the state resulting from the action indicated by the verb is still continuing:

① 窓が 割れて います。　　The window is broken.

② 電気が ついて います。　　The light is on.

Sentence ①, for example, indicates that the window broke at a certain time in the past and that the result (i.e. the broken-window situation) continues even now.

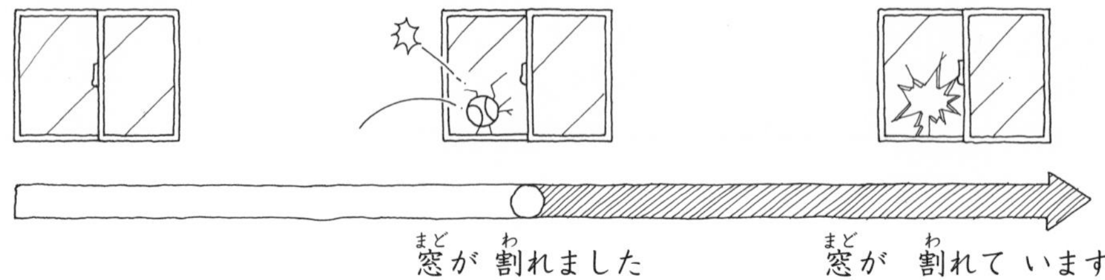


Verbs that can be used in this way include あきます, しまります, つきます, きえます, こわれます, われます, and others where a change takes place, and a different state is produced, as a result of the action indicated by the verb.

When describing a situation in front of one's eyes as a whole, the subject is indicated by が as in examples ① and ②. When introducing the subject as the topic, the particle は is used as in example ③:



③ この いすは 壊れて います。　　This chair is broken.

### 2. V て -form しまいました／しまいます

～て しまいました emphasises that an action has been completed. ～て しまいます indicates that an action will be completed at some point in the future:

④ シュミットさんが 持って 来た ワインは みんなで 飲んで しまいました。
We drank up all the wine that Mr. Schmidt brought.

⑤ 漢字の 宿題は もう やって しまいました。
I've already completed my kanji homework.

⑥ 昼ごはんまでに レポートを 書いて しまいます。
I'll finish writing my report by lunchtime.

～て しまいました may also indicate a feeling of regret or disappointment on the part of the speaker, as in examples ⑦ and ⑧:

⑦ パスポートを なくして しまいました。　　I went and lost my passport.

⑧ パソコンが 故障して しまいました。　　My PC went and broke down.

### 3. N(place)に 行きます／来ます／帰ります

In ⑨ (see Exercise C3), the particle に (indicating an arrival point) is used instead of the particle へ (indicating a direction). Verbs such as いきます, きます and かえります can be used with either 'place へ' or 'place に' in this way:

⑨ どこかで 財布(さいふ)を 落(お)として しまったんです。
……それは 大変(たいへん)ですね。すぐ 交番(こうばん)に 行(い)かないと。
I've gone and dropped my wallet somewhere.
…… Oh dear. We must go to the police box right away.

## 4. それ／その／そう

Lesson 2 explained how to use demonstratives to point to something tangible. The present lesson introduces the use of それ , その , and そう to indicate something appearing in speech or writing.

1) In speech

それ in Examples ⑩ and ⑪, その in Example ⑫, and そう in Example ⑬ point to what someone has just said:

⑩ どこかで 財布(さいふ)を 落(お)として しまったんです。
……それは 大変(たいへん)ですね。すぐ 交番(こうばん)に 行(い)かないと。
I've gone and dropped my wallet somewhere.
…… Oh dear. We must go to the police box right away.

⑪ 来月(らいげつ)から 大阪(おおさか)の 本社(ほんしゃ)に 転勤(てんきん)なんです。
I'm moving to Head Office in Osaka next month.
……それは おめでとう ございます。　……Congratulations! (See Lesson 31)

⑫ あのう、途中(とちゅう)で やめたい 場合(ばあい)は？
……その 場合(ばあい)は、近(ちか)くの 係員(かかりいん)に 名前(なまえ)を 言(い)って、帰(かえ)って ください。
Er... What do we do if we want to stop in the middle?
…… In that case, please give your name to a nearby official and then go home. (See Lesson 45)

⑬ うちへ 帰(かえ)って、休(やす)んだ ほうが いいですよ。　You'd better go home and take it easy.
……ええ、そう します。　……Yes, I will. (See Lesson 32)

2) In writing

The その in Example ⑭ indicates something that appeared in the previous sentence:

⑭ 一人(ひとり)で コンサートや 展覧会(てんらんかい)に 出(で)かけると、いいでしょう。その とき 会(あ)った 人(ひと)が 将来(しょうらい)の 恋人(こいびと)に なるかも しれません。
It's probably a good thing to go to concerts and exhibitions on your own. Someone you meet there might become your lover in the future. (See Lesson 32)

## 5. ありました

⑮ ［かばんが］ありましたよ。　Here's your bag!

This ありました indicates that the speaker has just found the bag. It does not mean 'a bag used to be here before'.

## 6. どこかで／どこかに

The particle へ or を after どこか or なにか can be omitted, but the particle で or に cannot:

⑯ どこかで 財布(さいふ)を なくして しまいました。　I've gone and lost my wallet somewhere.

⑰ どこかに 電話(でんわ)が ありますか。　Is there a telephone somewhere around here?

# Lesson 30

## I. Vocabulary

| | | |
|---|---|---|
| はりますⅠ | | put up, post, paste |
| かけますⅡ | 掛けます | hang |
| かざりますⅠ | 飾ります | display, decorate |
| ならべますⅡ | 並べます | arrange, line up |
| うえますⅡ | 植えます | plant |
| もどしますⅠ | 戻します | return, put ～ back |
| まとめますⅡ | | put ～ together, put ～ in shape, sum up |
| しまいますⅠ | | put (things) away |
| きめますⅡ | 決めます | decide |
| よしゅうしますⅢ | 予習します | prepare one's lesson |
| ふくしゅうしますⅢ | 復習します | review one's lesson |
| そのままに しますⅢ | | leave things as they are |
| じゅぎょう | 授業 | class |
| こうぎ | 講義 | lecture |
| ミーティング | | meeting |
| よてい | 予定 | plan, schedule |
| おしらせ | お知らせ | notice |
| ガイドブック | | guidebook |
| カレンダー | | calendar |
| ポスター | | poster |
| よていひょう | 予定表 | schedule |
| ごみばこ | ごみ箱 | trash can, dustbin |
| にんぎょう | 人形 | doll |
| かびん | 花瓶 | vase |
| かがみ | 鏡 | mirror |
| ひきだし | 引き出し | drawer |
| げんかん | 玄関 | front door, porch, entrance hall |
| ろうか | 廊下 | corridor, hallway |
| かべ | 壁 | wall |
| いけ | 池 | pond |
| もとの ところ | 元の 所 | original place |
| まわり | 周り | round, around |
| まんなか* | 真ん中 | centre |
| すみ | 隅 | corner |
| まだ | | still |

### 〈会話（かいわ）〉

| | |
|---|---|
| リュック | rucksack |
| 非常袋（ひじょうぶくろ） | emergency kit |
| 非常時（ひじょうじ） | emergency |
| 生活（せいかつ）しますⅢ | live |
| 懐中電灯（かいちゅうでんとう） | torch, flashlight |
| ～とか、～とか | ～, ～, and so on |

### 〈読み物（よみもの）〉

| | |
|---|---|
| 丸（まる）い | round |
| ある ～ | one ～, a certain ～ |
| 夢（ゆめ）を 見（み）ますⅡ | dream |
| うれしい | glad, happy |
| 嫌（いや）[な] | hateful, disagreeable |
| すると | and, then |
| 目（め）が 覚（さ）めますⅡ | wake up |

## II. Translation

### Sentence Patterns

1. There's a street map on the wall of the police box.
2. I'll check things out on the Internet before the trip.

### Example Sentences

1. The new station toilets are interesting, aren't they?
   ······Oh? Are they?
   The walls are painted with pictures of flowers and animals.
2. Where's the Sellotape?
   ······It's in that drawer.
3. About next month's business trip....shall I book the hotel?
   ······Yes, please.
4. When you've finished using the scissors, please put them back where they came from.
   ······Yes, I will.
5. May I tidy up the papers?
   ······No, please leave them as they are.
   I'm still using them.





### Conversation

**I must get myself an emergency kit**

Miller: Hello.
Suzuki: Welcome. Please come in.
Miller: That's a big rucksack there.
Are you off to the mountains?
Suzuki: No, it's my emergency kit.
Miller: An emergency kit? What's that?
Suzuki: It's a bag with everything you need in it for an emergency.
I can live for three days with what's in it, even if the gas and electricity are cut off.
Miller: Is it water and food?
Suzuki: Yes, and various other things as well, like a torch and a radio......
Miller: I must get one ready for myself.
Suzuki: They sell emergency kits in supermarkets, you know.
Miller: Oh, do they? In that case, I'll buy one.

## III. Useful Words & Information

### 非常の場合　Emergency

〔1〕地震の場合　In Case of an Earthquake

1）備えが大切　Preparation is Important

① 家具が倒れないようにしておく
Fix furniture so that it will not fall over.

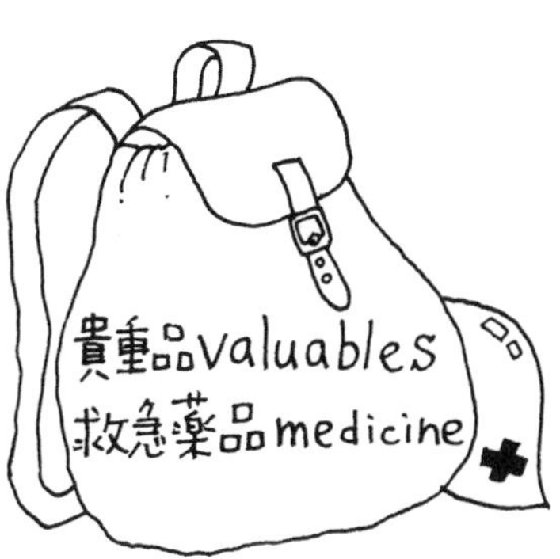


② 消火器を備える・水を貯えておく
Have a fire extinguisher on hand, and keep an emergency supply of water ready.

③ 非常袋を用意しておく
Have an emergency kit ready.

④ 地域の避難場所を確認しておく
Make sure you know where your district's evacuation point is.

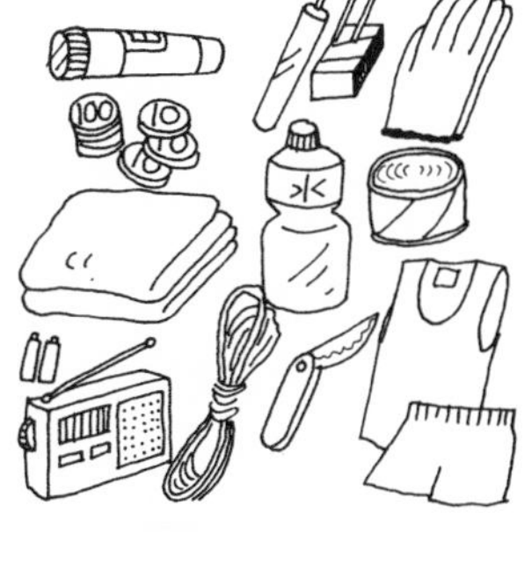

⑤ 家族、知人、友人と、もしもの場合の連絡先を決めておく
Decide on a contact address with your family, friends and acquaintances.

2）万一地震が起きた場合　When an Earthquake Strikes

① 丈夫なテーブルの下にもぐる
Get under a sturdy table.

② 落ち着いて火の始末
Calmly extinguish any fire.

③ 戸を開けて出口の確保
Open doors to secure an exit path.

④ 慌てて外に飛び出さない
Do not panic or rush outside.

3）地震が収まったら　When the Earthquake Stops

正しい情報を聞く（山崩れ、崖崩れ、津波に注意）
Get accurate information (beware of landslides and tidal waves).

4）避難する場合は　When Evacuating

車を使わず、必ず歩いて
Do not evacuate by car; always leave on foot.

〔2〕台風の場合　In Case of a Typhoon

| | |
|---|---|
| ① 気象情報を聞く | Listen to the weather forecast. |
| ② 家の周りの点検 | Check the exterior of the house. |
| ③ ラジオの電池の備えを | Have radio batteries on hand. |
| ④ 水、緊急食品の準備 | Have a supply of water and food ready. |

## IV. Grammar Notes

### 1. V て -form あります

V て -form あります indicates a continuing state resulting from a purposeful action. Transitive verbs are used for this:

1) $N_1$ に $N_2$ が V て -form あります

① 机の 上に メモが 置いて あります。

Someone's left a note on the desk.

② カレンダーに 今月の 予定が 書いて あります。

This month's schedule is written on the calendar.

2) $N_2$ は $N_1$ に V て -form あります

When $N_2$ is taken as the topic, it is indicated by the particle は :

③ メモは どこですか。

…… ［メモは］ 机の 上に 置いて あります。

Where's the note?

…… [The note is] on the desk.

④ 今月の 予定は カレンダーに 書いて あります。

This month's schedule is written on the calendar.

[Note] The difference between V て -form います and V て -form あります :

⑤ 窓が 閉まって います。　　The window is shut.

⑥ 窓が 閉めて あります。　　The window has been shut.

Examples ⑤ and ⑥ illustrate the use of an intransitive verb ( しまります ) and its corresponding transitive verb ( しめます ) with V て -form います and V て -form あります respectively. Example ⑤ simply indicates that the situation exists (i.e. that the window is shut), while Example ⑥ emphasises that the situation exists as a result of somebody's deliberate action, i.e., that the window is shut because somebody deliberately shut it.

### 2. V て -form おきます

1) This can indicate that a necessary action or behaviour is to be performed by a certain time:

⑦ 旅行の まえに、切符を 買って おきます。

I'll buy my tickets before travelling.

⑧ 次の 会議までに 何を して おいたら いいですか。

……この 資料を 読んで おいて ください。

What should I do before the next meeting?

…… Please read these documents.

2) It can indicate taking some temporary measures or completing a necessary action in preparation for the next time one uses something:

⑨ はさみを 使ったら、元の 所に 戻して おいて ください。

When you've finished using the scissors, please put them back where they were.

3) It indicates keeping a resultant state as it is:

⑩ あした 会議(かいぎ)が ありますから、いすは この ままに して おいて ください。

There's a meeting here tomorrow, so please leave the chairs as they are.

[Note] In speech, ～て おきます often becomes ～ときます:

⑪ そこに 置(お)いといて（置(お)いて おいて）ください。

Please leave it there. (See Lesson 38)

**3.** **まだ＋ affirmative** still

⑫ まだ 雨(あめ)が 降(ふ)って います。　It's still raining.

⑬ 道具(どうぐ)を 片(かた)づけましょうか。

……まだ 使(つか)って いますから、その ままに して おいて ください。

Shall I put the tools away?

…… No, I'm still using them; please leave them where they are.

まだ ('yet' or 'still') is used here to indicate that an action or situation is continuing.

**4.** **とか**

とか is used in the same way as や in listing instances of something. It is more colloquial than や and may also be used after the final noun on a list:

⑭ どんな スポーツを して いますか。

……そうですね。テニスとか 水泳(すいえい)とか……。

What sports do you do?

…… Yes, well...tennis, swimming, and so on......

**5.** **Particle ＋も**

When も is attached to a noun to which が or を is already attached, it replaces these. When another particle (such as に, で, から, まで or と) is already attached to the noun, that particle is left in place and も is appended to it. If the other particle is へ, then も may either replace it or be appended to it.

⑮ ほかにも いろいろ あります。　There are various other things as well.

⑯ どこ[へ]も 行(い)きません。　I'm not going anywhere.

# Lesson 31

## I. Vocabulary

| | | |
|---|---|---|
| つづけますⅡ | 続けます | continue |
| みつけますⅡ | 見つけます | find |
| とりますⅠ<br>［やすみを～］ | 取ります<br>［休みを～］ | take [a holiday] |
| うけますⅡ<br>［しけんを～］ | 受けます<br>［試験を～］ | take [an examination] |
| もうしこみますⅠ | 申し込みます | apply for, enter for |
| きゅうけいしますⅢ | 休憩します | take a break, take a rest |
| | | |
| れんきゅう | 連休 | consecutive holidays |
| | | |
| さくぶん | 作文 | essay, composition |
| はっぴょう | 発表 | announcement, presentation（～します：announce） |
| | | |
| てんらんかい | 展覧会 | exhibition |
| けっこんしき | 結婚式 | wedding ceremony |
| ［お］そうしき* | ［お］葬式 | funeral |
| しき* | 式 | ceremony |
| | | |
| ほんしゃ | 本社 | head office |
| してん | 支店 | branch office |
| きょうかい | 教会 | church |
| だいがくいん | 大学院 | graduate school |
| どうぶつえん | 動物園 | zoo |
| おんせん | 温泉 | hot spring, spa |
| | | |
| かえり | 帰り | return |
| | | |
| おこさん | お子さん | （someone else's） child |
| | | |
| －ごう | －号 | （train number, typhoon number, etc.） |
| | | |
| ～の ほう | ～の 方 | place toward ～, direction of ～ |
| | | |
| ずっと | | the whole time |
| | | |
| ※バリ | | Bali（Indonesian island） |
| ※ピカソ | | Pablo Picasso, Spanish painter（1881-1973） |
| ※のぞみ | | name of a Shinkansen train（～42号（ごう）：Nozomi Superexpress No.42） |
| ※新神戸（しんこうべ） | | name of a station in Hyogo prefecture |

### 〈会話(かいわ)〉

| | |
|---|---|
| 残(のこ)りますⅠ | remain, be left, stay behind |
| 入学試験(にゅうがくしけん) | entrance examination |
| 月(つき)に | per month |

### 〈読(よ)み物(もの)〉

| | |
|---|---|
| 村(むら) | village |
| 卒業(そつぎょう)しますⅢ | graduate |
| 映画館(えいがかん) | movie theater, cinema |
| 嫌(いや)[な] | hateful, disagreeable |
| 空(そら) | sky |
| 閉(と)じますⅡ | close |
| 都会(とかい) | city |
| 子(こ)どもたち | children |
| 自由(じゆう)に | freely |

## II. Translation

### Sentence Patterns

1. Let's go together.
2. I'm thinking of setting up my own company in the future.
3. I intend to buy a car next month.

### Example Sentences

1. I'm tired. Shall we rest for a bit?
   ……Yes, let's do that.
2. What are you going to do at New Year?
   ……I'm thinking of going to a hot spring with my family.
3. Have you finished your report already?
   ……No, I haven't written it yet.
   I'm planning to finish it by Friday.
4. Will you carry on studying Japanese even after you've gone back to your home country?
   ……Yes, I intend to continue.
5. Aren't you going back to your home country for the summer holidays?
   ……No, I'll be taking my graduate school entrance exam, so I'm not planning to go home this year.
6. I'm going on a business trip to New York tomorrow.
   ……Are you? When are you coming back?
   I'm scheduled to come back next Friday.





### Conversation

**I'm thinking of learning how to cook**

Ogawa: I'm going to be single from next month.
Miller: What do you mean?
Ogawa: As a matter of fact, I'm being transferred to the Head Office in Osaka.
Miller: The Head Office? Congratulations.
But why will you be single?
Ogawa: My wife and son are staying behind in Tokyo.
Miller: Really, aren't they going with you?
Ogawa: No. My son says he wants to stay in Tokyo because he's taking his university entrance exams next year, and my wife says she doesn't want to leave the company she's working at.
Miller: So you're going to live apart?
Ogawa: Yes, but I'm planning to come home for two or three weekends a month.
Miller: Tough, isn't it?
Ogawa: Yes, but it's a good opportunity. I'm thinking of learning how to cook.
Miller: That's good.

## III. Useful Words & Information

### 専門（せんもん） Fields of Study

| | | |
|---|---|---|
| 医学 | いがく | medical science |
| 薬学 | やくがく | pharmacology |
| 化学 | かがく | chemistry |
| 生化学 | せいかがく | biochemistry |
| 生物学 | せいぶつがく | biology |
| 農学 | のうがく | agriculture |
| 地学 | ちがく | geology |
| 地理学 | ちりがく | geography |
| 数学 | すうがく | mathematics |
| 物理学 | ぶつりがく | physics |
| 工学 | こうがく | engineering |
| 土木工学 | どぼくこうがく | civil engineering |
| 電子工学 | でんしこうがく | electronics |
| 電気工学 | でんきこうがく | electrical engineering |
| 機械工学 | きかいこうがく | mechanical engineering |
| コンピューター工学 | こうがく | computer science |
| 遺伝子工学 | いでんしこうがく | genetic engineering |
| 建築学 | けんちくがく | architecture |
| 天文学 | てんもんがく | astronomy |
| 環境科学 | かんきょうかがく | environmental science |
| 政治学 | せいじがく | politics |
| 国際関係学 | こくさいかんけいがく | international relations |
| 法律学 | ほうりつがく | law |
| 経済学 | けいざいがく | economics |
| 経営学 | けいえいがく | business administration |
| 社会学 | しゃかいがく | sociology |
| 教育学 | きょういくがく | education |
| 文学 | ぶんがく | literature |
| 言語学 | げんごがく | linguistics |
| 心理学 | しんりがく | psychology |
| 哲学 | てつがく | philosophy |
| 宗教学 | しゅうきょうがく | religious studies |
| 芸術 | げいじゅつ | arts |
| 美術 | びじゅつ | fine arts |
| 音楽 | おんがく | music |
| 体育学 | たいいくがく | physical education |

# IV. Grammar Notes

## 1. Volitional form

The ます -form is changed into the volitional form as follows (see Exercise A1, Lesson 31, Main Text).

Group I: Change the い -column sound that is the final sound of the ます -form to the お -column sound and add う :

かきーます → かこーう　　いそぎーます → いそごーう
よみーます → よもーう　　あそびーます → あそぼーう

Group II: Attach よう to the ます -form:

たべーます → たべーよう　　みーます → みーよう

Group III:

しーます → しーよう　　きーます → こーよう

## 2. Uses of the volitional form

1) In plain-style sentences as the plain form of ～ましょう :

| | | |
|---|---|---|
| ① | ちょっと 休まない？<br>……うん、休もう。 | Shall we take a quick break?<br>……Yes, let's. |
| ② | 手伝おうか。 | May I help? |
| ③ | 傘を 持って 行こうか。 | Shall we take our umbrellas? |

[Note] Although plain-style questions do not usually take the particle か on their end, it is required with questions using the plain form of ～ましょうか, as in Examples ② and ③ .

2) V volitional form と 思って います

This sentence pattern is used to convey the speaker's intention to the listener. V volitional form と おもいます can also be used with the same meaning, but V volitional form と おもって います indicates that the speaker made the decision some time ago:

④ 週末は 海へ 行こうと 思って います。

I'm thinking of going to the seaside at the weekend.

⑤ 今から 銀行へ 行こうと 思います。

I think I'll go to the bank now.

[Note] V volitional form と おもいます can only be used to convey the speaker's intention, but V volitional form と おもって います can also be used to indicate a third party's intention:

⑥ 彼は 学校を 作ろうと 思って います。

He's thinking of setting up a school.

## 3. V dictionary form / V ない -form ない } つもりです

V dictionary form つもりです expresses the speaker's intention to do something. To indicate an intention not to do something, V ない -form ない つもりです is usually used.

⑦ 国へ 帰っても、日本語の 勉強を 続ける つもりです。

I intend to continue studying Japanese even after I have returned to my home country.

## III. Useful Words & Information

### 専門（せんもん） Fields of Study

| | |
|---|---|
| 医学（いがく） | medical science |
| 薬学（やくがく） | pharmacology |
| 化学（かがく） | chemistry |
| 生化学（せいかがく） | biochemistry |
| 生物学（せいぶつがく） | biology |
| 農学（のうがく） | agriculture |
| 地学（ちがく） | geology |
| 地理学（ちりがく） | geography |
| 数学（すうがく） | mathematics |
| 物理学（ぶつりがく） | physics |
| 工学（こうがく） | engineering |
| 土木工学（どぼくこうがく） | civil engineering |
| 電子工学（でんしこうがく） | electronics |
| 電気工学（でんきこうがく） | electrical engineering |
| 機械工学（きかいこうがく） | mechanical engineering |
| コンピューター工学（こうがく） | computer science |
| 遺伝子工学（いでんしこうがく） | genetic engineering |
| 建築学（けんちくがく） | architecture |
| 天文学（てんもんがく） | astronomy |
| 環境科学（かんきょうかがく） | environmental science |
| 政治学（せいじがく） | politics |
| 国際関係学（こくさいかんけいがく） | international relations |
| 法律学（ほうりつがく） | law |
| 経済学（けいざいがく） | economics |
| 経営学（けいえいがく） | business administration |
| 社会学（しゃかいがく） | sociology |
| 教育学（きょういくがく） | education |
| 文学（ぶんがく） | literature |
| 言語学（げんごがく） | linguistics |
| 心理学（しんりがく） | psychology |
| 哲学（てつがく） | philosophy |
| 宗教学（しゅうきょうがく） | religious studies |
| 芸術（げいじゅつ） | arts |
| 美術（びじゅつ） | fine arts |
| 音楽（おんがく） | music |
| 体育学（たいいくがく） | physical education |

⑧ あしたからは たばこを 吸わない つもりです。

I intend not to smoke from tomorrow on.

[Note] There is little difference in meaning between V volitional form と おもって います and V dictionary form つもりです, but the latter sounds more determined.

**4.** | V dictionary form / Nの } 予定です |

This is a way of stating something one plans to do:

⑨ 7月の 終わりに ドイツへ 出張する 予定です。

I plan to go to Germany on business at the end of July.

⑩ 旅行は 1週間ぐらいの 予定です。

The trip is scheduled to last for about a week.

**5.** | まだ V て-form いません |

This expression indicates that a situation has not yet occurred, or something has not yet been done:

⑪ 銀行は まだ 開いて いません。 The bank isn't open yet.

⑫ レポートは もう 書きましたか。

……いいえ、まだ 書いて いません。

Have you written the report yet?

…… No, I haven't.

**6.** | 帰ります ― 帰り |

The same form as the ます-form can be used as a noun, as in Examples ⑬ and ⑭:

⑬ 帰りの 新幹線は どこから 乗りますか。

Where do we get on the Shinkansen to go back?

⑭ 休みは 何曜日ですか。 Which days do you have off? (See Lesson 4)

In addition, the following also exist:

遊びます ― 遊び　　答えます ― 答え

申し込みます ― 申し込み　　楽しみます (enjoy) ― 楽しみ

# Lesson 32

## I. Vocabulary

| | | |
|---|---|---|
| うんどうしますⅢ | 運動します | (take) exercise |
| せいこうしますⅢ | 成功します | succeed |
| しっぱいしますⅢ* | 失敗します | fail [an examination] |
| [しけんに～] | [試験に～] | |
| ごうかくしますⅢ | 合格します | pass [an examination] |
| [しけんに～] | [試験に～] | |
| やみますⅠ | | [rain] stop |
| [あめが～] | [雨が～] | |
| はれますⅡ | 晴れます | clear up |
| くもりますⅠ | 曇ります | get cloudy |
| つづきますⅠ | 続きます | [high temperature/fever] continue |
| [ねつが～] | [熱が～] | |
| ひきますⅠ | | catch [a cold] |
| [かぜを～] | | |
| ひやしますⅠ | 冷やします | cool |
| こみますⅠ | 込みます | [a road] get crowded |
| [みちが～] | [道が～] | |
| すきますⅠ | | [a road] get less crowded |
| [みちが～] | [道が～] | |
| でますⅡ | 出ます | |
| [しあいに～] | [試合に～] | participate [in the match] |
| [パーティーに～] | | attend [a party] |
| むりを しますⅢ | 無理を します | overdo things |
| じゅうぶん[な] | 十分[な] | enough, sufficient |
| おかしい | | strange, funny |
| うるさい | | noisy |
| せんせい | 先生 | doctor |
| やけど | | burning (～を します：get burned) |
| けが | | injury (～を します：get injured) |
| せき | | cough (～を します／～が でます：have a cough) |
| インフルエンザ | | influenza |
| そら | 空 | sky |
| たいよう* | 太陽 | sun |
| ほし | 星 | star |
| かぜ | 風 | wind |
| ひがし* | 東 | east |
| にし | 西 | west |
| みなみ | 南 | south |
| きた* | 北 | north |

| | | |
|---|---|---|
| こくさい～ | 国際～ | international ～ |
| すいどう | 水道 | faucet, tap, water supply |
| エンジン | | engine |
| チーム | | team |
| こんや | 今夜 | this evening |
| ゆうがた | 夕方 | late afternoon |
| まえ | | a time in the past, before |
| おそく | 遅く | late (time) |
| こんなに* | | this (much, etc.) |
| そんなに* | | that (much, etc.) (concerning a matter related to the listener) |
| あんなに | | that (much, etc.) (concerning a matter not related to the speaker or the listener) |
| ※ヨーロッパ | | Europe |

**〈会話(かいわ)〉**

| | |
|---|---|
| 元気(げんき) | vigour |
| 胃(い) | stomach |
| ストレス | stress |
| それは いけませんね。 | I'm sorry to hear that. |

**〈読み物(よみもの)〉**

| | |
|---|---|
| 星占い(ほしうらない) | horoscope |
| 牡牛座(おうしざ) | Taurus |
| 働き(はたら)すぎ | overworking |
| 困(こま)りますⅠ | be in trouble, have a problem |
| 宝(たから)くじ | lottery |
| 当(あ)たりますⅠ ［宝(たから)くじが～］ | win [a lottery] |
| 健康(けんこう) | health |
| 恋愛(れんあい) | romantic love |
| 恋人(こいびと) | sweetheart, boyfriend, girlfriend |
| ラッキーアイテム | something lucky |
| 石(いし) | stone |

## II. Translation

### Sentence Patterns

1. It's better to exercise every day.
2. It'll probably snow tomorrow.
3. I may not make it in time.

### Example Sentences

1. What do you think about students having part-time jobs?
   ……I think it's fine. It's good to have a variety of experiences while you're young.
2. I'd like to go travelling in Europe for about a month; do you think four hundred thousand yen will be enough?
   ……I think that would be plenty, but it would be better not to take it in cash.
3. Professor, what do you think will happen to the Japanese economy?
   ……Hmm...it probably won't improve for a while yet.
4. Doctor, has Hans got the flu?
   ……Yes, it's influenza. He may have a high temperature for two or three days, but there's no need to worry.
5. The engine sounds funny, doesn't it?
   ……Yes, it does. It might break down.
   Let's check it out.





### Conversation

**It's better not to overdo things**

Ogawa: You don't look too good, Mr. Schmidt.
What's the matter?

Schmidt: I haven't been feeling very well lately.
My head and stomach sometimes hurt.

Ogawa: That won't do, will it? Are you very busy at work?

Schmidt: Yes, I'm having to do a lot of overtime.

Ogawa: It could be stress, couldn't it?
You'd better have a checkup at the hospital.

Schmidt: Yes, you're right.

Ogawa: It's better not to overdo things, you know.

Schmidt: Yes, I'm thinking of taking a holiday when I've finished the job I'm working on.

Ogawa: That'd be good.

## III. Useful Words & Information

### 天気予報（てんきよほう） Weather Forecast

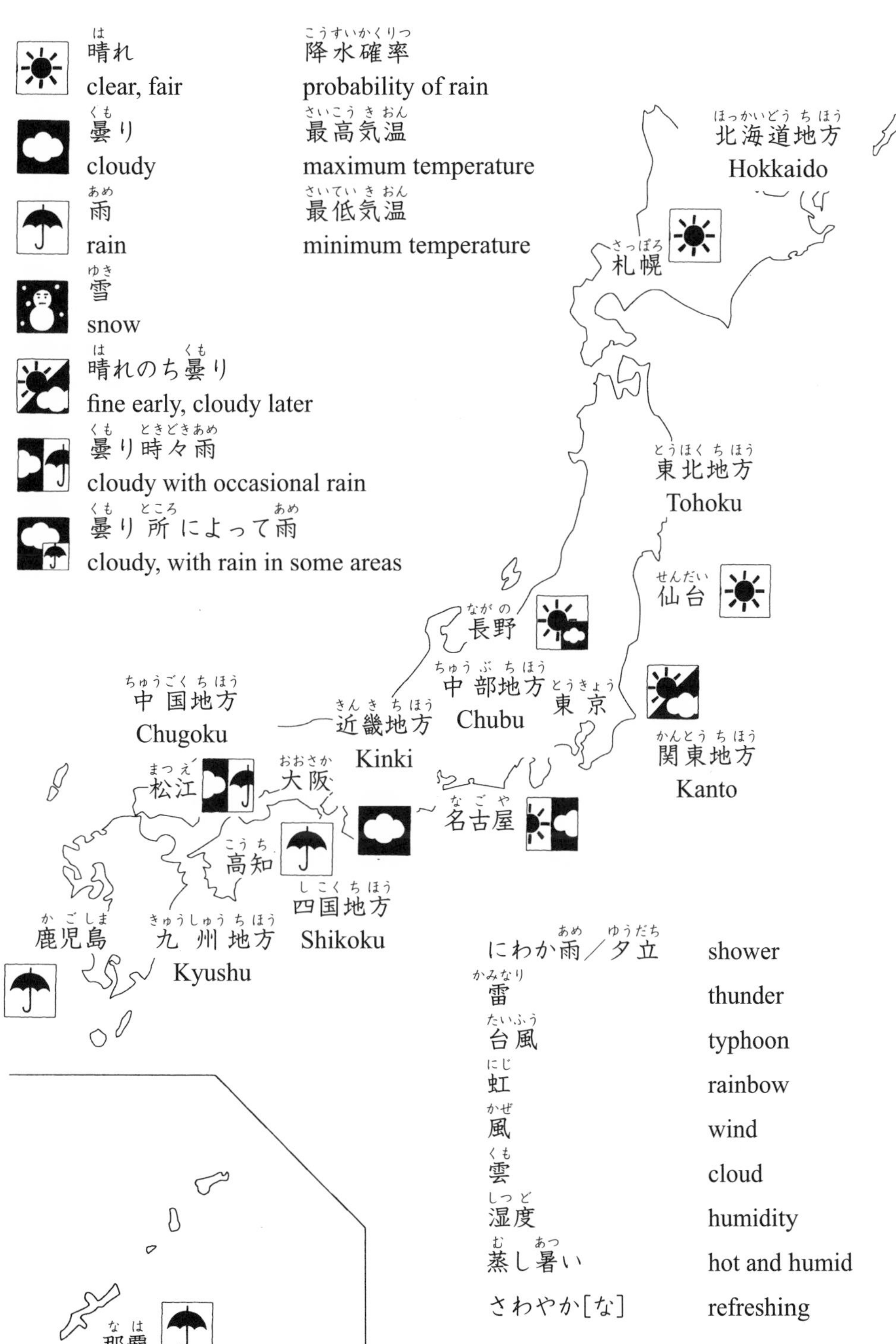


| | |
|---|---|
| 晴れ（はれ） | clear, fair |
| 曇り（くもり） | cloudy |
| 雨（あめ） | rain |
| 雪（ゆき） | snow |
| 晴れのち曇り（はれのちくもり） | fine early, cloudy later |
| 曇り時々雨（くもりときどきあめ） | cloudy with occasional rain |
| 曇り所によって雨（くもりところによってあめ） | cloudy, with rain in some areas |
| 降水確率（こうすいかくりつ） | probability of rain |
| 最高気温（さいこうきおん） | maximum temperature |
| 最低気温（さいていきおん） | minimum temperature |

| | |
|---|---|
| にわか雨（あめ）／夕立（ゆうだち） | shower |
| 雷（かみなり） | thunder |
| 台風（たいふう） | typhoon |
| 虹（にじ） | rainbow |
| 風（かぜ） | wind |
| 雲（くも） | cloud |
| 湿度（しつど） | humidity |
| 蒸し暑い（むしあつい） | hot and humid |
| さわやか［な］ | refreshing |

## IV. Grammar Notes

**1.**

| | | |
|---|---|---|
| **V た -form** | } | ほうが　いいです |
| **V ない -form ない** | | |

① 毎日　運動した　ほうが　いいです。

You'd better take some exercise every day.

② 熱が　あるんです。

……じゃ、おふろに　入らない　ほうが　いいですよ。

I've got a temperature.

…… In that case, you'd better not have a bath.

This sentence pattern is used to make suggestions or give advice. Since V た -form ほうが いいです includes the meaning of comparing two things and selecting one of them, it implies that it would be bad not to take the action specified by the verb. Because of this, it may give the impression that the speaker is being overbearing. When simply recommending a certain action, ～たら　いい (see Lesson 26) is used:

③ 日本の　お寺が　見たいんですが……。

……じゃ、京都へ　行ったら　いいですよ。

I'd like to see some Japanese temples......

…… In that case, it would be good to go to Kyoto.

**2.**

| | | |
|---|---|---|
| **V** / **い -adj** | **plain form** | でしょう |
| **な -adj** / **N** | **plain form** ～だ | |

～でしょう is used when a speaker wants to express an opinion about something in the future or something uncertain, without being definite:

④ あしたは　雨が　降るでしょう。

It will probably rain tomorrow.

⑤ タワポンさんは　合格するでしょうか。

……きっと　合格するでしょう。

I wonder whether Thawaphon will pass?

…… I'm sure he will.

**3.**

| | | |
|---|---|---|
| **V** / **い -adj** | **plain form** | かも　しれません |
| **な -adj** / **N** | **plain form** ～だ | |

～かも　しれません can be used when the speaker wants to point out that there is a possibility, however small, of ～:

⑥ 約束の　時間に　間に　合わないかも　しれません。

We might not get there in time for the appointment.

### 4. V ます -form ましょう

⑦ エンジンの 音(おと)が おかしいんですが。
……そうですね。故障(こしょう)かも しれません。ちょっと 調(しら)べましょう。
The engine sounds funny......
…… You're right. It might have broken down. Let me check it.

The V ます -form ましょう in Example ⑦ is an expression used to convey the speaker's intention to the listener, and is used when announcing an action. It has a more assertive tone than V ます -form ましょうか (see Lesson 14).

### 5. Quantifier で

This shows a time limit or other limit:

⑧ 駅(えき)まで 30分(ぷん)で 行(い)けますか。
Can we get to the station in thirty minutes?

⑨ 3万円(まんえん)で パソコンが 買(か)えますか。
Can you buy a PC for 30,000 yen?

### 6. 何(なに)か 心配(しんぱい)な こと

⑩ 何(なに)か 心配(しんぱい)な ことが あるんですか。
Is there anything you're worried about?

In a case like that illustrated in Example ⑩, the expression なにか しんぱいな こと is used, not しんぱいな なにか. Other expressions such as なにか ～ もの, どこか ～ ところ, だれか ～ ひと, いつか ～ とき are also used:

⑪ スキーに 行(い)きたいんですが、どこか いい 所(ところ)、ありますか。
I want to go skiing; can you recommend somewhere good?

# Lesson 33

## I. Vocabulary

| | | |
|---|---|---|
| にげますⅡ | 逃げます | run away |
| さわぎますⅠ | 騒ぎます | make a noise |
| あきらめますⅡ | | give up |
| なげますⅡ | 投げます | throw |
| まもりますⅠ | 守ります | keep, follow, obey |
| はじまりますⅠ | 始まります | [a ceremony] begin, start |
| ［しきが～］ | ［式が～］ | |
| しゅっせきしますⅢ | 出席します | attend [a meeting] |
| ［かいぎに～］ | ［会議に～］ | |
| つたえますⅡ | 伝えます | convey |
| ちゅういしますⅢ | 注意します | be careful [of the cars] |
| ［くるまに～］ | ［車に～］ | |
| はずしますⅠ | 外します | be away [from one's desk] |
| ［せきを～］ | ［席を～］ | |
| もどりますⅠ | 戻ります | come back, return |
| ありますⅠ | | have [a telephone call] |
| ［でんわが～］ | ［電話が～］ | |
| リサイクルしますⅢ | | recycle |
| だめ［な］ | | no good, not permitted, impossible |
| おなじ | 同じ | same |
| けいさつ | 警察 | police (station) |
| せき | 席 | seat |
| マーク | | mark, symbol |
| ボール | | ball |
| しめきり | 締め切り | deadline |
| きそく | 規則 | regulation, rule |
| きけん | 危険 | Danger |
| しようきんし | 使用禁止 | Do Not Use |
| たちいりきんし | 立入禁止 | Keep Out |
| じょこう | 徐行 | Go Slow |
| いりぐち | 入口 | entrance |
| でぐち | 出口 | exit |
| ひじょうぐち | 非常口 | emergency exit |
| むりょう | 無料 | Free of Charge |
| わりびき | 割引 | Discount |
| のみほうだい | 飲み放題 | All You Can Drink |
| しようちゅう | 使用中 | In Use |
| ぼしゅうちゅう | 募集中 | Applications Wanted |

33

| | | |
|---|---|---|
| ～ちゅう | ～中 | -ing |
| どういう ～ | | what (kind of ～) |
| いくら [～ても] | | however ～, even if ～ |
| もう | | (not) any longer (used with negatives) |
| あと ～ | | ～ left |
| ～ほど | | about ～ |

**〈会話（かいわ）〉**

| | |
|---|---|
| 駐車違反（ちゅうしゃいはん） | parking violation |
| 罰金（ばっきん） | fine |

**〈読み物（よみもの）〉**

| | |
|---|---|
| 地震（じしん） | earthquake |
| 起（お）きますII | happen |
| 助（たす）け合（あ）いますI | help each other |
| もともと | originally |
| 悲（かな）しい | sad |
| もっと | more |
| あいさつ | greeting, address (～を します: greet, give an address) |
| 相手（あいて） | the other person |
| 気持（きも）ち | feeling |

## II. Translation

### Sentence Patterns

1. Hurry up!
2. Don't touch!
3. 'Tachiiri Kinshi' means 'No Entry'.
4. Mr. Miller said he was going to Osaka on business next week.

### Example Sentences

1. It's no good. I can't run any more.
   ……Come on! It's only another five hundred metres!
2. There's no time left.
   ……There's still a minute left. Don't give up!
3. You can't play in this pond. There's a sign saying, 'No Entry' over there.
   ……Oh, so there is.
4. How do you read those kanji?
   ……They say 'Kin'en'.
   It means 'No Smoking'.
5. What does this symbol mean?
   ……It means that you can wash it in a washing machine.
6. Is Mr. Gupta here?
   ……No, he's out at the moment. He said he'd be back in about thirty minutes.
7. Excuse me, but would you mind telling Ms. Watanabe that the party tomorrow will start at six o'clock?
   ……Got it. Six o'clock, right?





### Conversation

**What does this mean?**

Watt: Excuse me, this piece of paper was stuck on my car. How do you read these kanji?
University Staff Member: It says, 'Chusha Ihan'.
Watt: 'Chusha Ihan'?.......What does that mean?
University Staff Member: It means that you parked your car somewhere you shouldn't have. Where did you park it?
Watt: In front of the station. Only for ten minutes, while I went to buy a magazine......
University Staff Member: You can't even park for ten minutes in front of a station.
Watt: Oh dear. Will I have to pay a fine?
University Staff Member: Yes, you'll have to pay fifteen thousand yen.
Watt: Fifteen thousand yen?
The magazine only cost three hundred......

## III. Useful Words & Information

### 標識（ひょうしき） Signs

営業中（えいぎょうちゅう）
Open [for Business]

準備中（じゅんびちゅう）
In Preparation

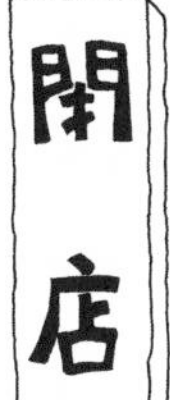


閉店（へいてん）
Closed

定休日（ていきゅうび）
Regular Holiday

化粧室（けしょうしつ）
Toilet

禁煙席（きんえんせき）
No-Smoking Seat

予約席（よやくせき）
Reserved Seat

非常口（ひじょうぐち）
Emergency Exit

火気厳禁（かきげんきん）
Flammable

割（わ）れ物（もの）注意（ちゅうい）
Fragile

運転初心者注意（うんてんしょしんしゃちゅうい）
New Driver

工事中（こうじちゅう）
Under Construction

塩素系漂白剤不可（えんそけいひょうはくざいふか）
Do not use chlorine-based bleach

手洗（てあら）い
Wash by hand

アイロン（低温（ていおん））
Cool iron

ドライクリーニング
Dry-clean only

# IV. Grammar Notes

## 1. Imperative and prohibitive forms

1) How to create the imperative form (See Exercise A1, Lesson 33, Main Text)

Group I: Change the い-column sound that is the final sound of the ます-form to the え-column sound:

かき－ます → かけ　　いそぎ－ます → いそげ
よみ－ます → よめ　　あそび－ます → あそべ

Group II: Attach ろ to the ます-form:

たべ－ます → たべ－ろ　　み－ます → み－ろ

Exception：くれ－ます → くれろ

Group III: し－ます → しろ　　き－ます → こい

[Note] State verbs such as ある, できる and わかる do not have an imperative form.

2) How to create the prohibitive form (See Exercise A1, Lesson 33, Main Text)

Add な to the dictionary form.

33

## 2. Uses of the imperative and prohibitive forms

The imperative form is used when demanding that the listener perform a certain action, and the prohibitive form is used when demanding that the listener not perform a certain action. Since they sound strongly coercive, they are very seldom used at the end of a sentence, and are used in speech almost exclusively by men. The imperative and prohibitive are used at the ends of sentences in the following types of situation:



1) By a man senior in age or status to someone who is his junior, or by a parent to their child:

① 早(はや)く 寝(ね)ろ。　Go to bed immediately!

② 遅(おく)れるな。　Don't be late!

2) Among male friends. The particle よ is often attached at the end of the sentence to soften the tone:

③ あした うちへ 来(こ)い[よ]。　Come to my house tomorrow, [won't you].

④ あまり 飲(の)むな[よ]。　[Hey,] don't drink too much!

3) When giving instructions to a group of people in a place like a factory; or during a fire, earthquake or other emergency, when there is no time to be polite. Even in such cases, they are often only used by men senior in age or status:

⑤ 逃(に)げろ。　Run!

⑥ エレベーターを 使(つか)うな。　Don't use the lift!

4) When giving commands during group training, a school physical education lesson, club sports activities and so on:

⑦ 休(やす)め。　At ease!

⑧ 休(やす)むな。　Don't slack!

5) When yelling encouragement at a sports event. Women sometimes also use these forms in such cases:

⑨ 頑張(がんば)れ。　Come on!

⑩ 負(ま)けるな。　Don't lose!

6) On traffic signs and in slogans, when brevity and impact are required:

⑪ 止(と)まれ。　　STOP

⑫ 入(はい)るな。　　NO ENTRY

[Note] V ます -form なさい is another type of imperative. It is used by a parent to their child or by a teacher to a pupil, and sounds softer than the imperative form of the verb. Women use this instead of the imperative form of the verb, but it cannot be used when addressing someone of superior status:

⑬ 勉強(べんきょう)しなさい。　　Go and study!

## 3. 〜と 書(か)いて あります／〜と 読(よ)みます

⑭ あの 漢字(かんじ)は 何(なん)と 読(よ)むんですか。　　How do you read that kanji?

⑮ あそこに「止(と)まれ」と 書(か)いて あります。　　It says, 'STOP' over there.

The と in Examples ⑭ and ⑮ has the same function as the と in 〜と いいます (see Lesson 21).

## 4. X は Y と いう 意味(いみ)です

This form is used when defining X. と いう comes from と いいます. When inquiring as to the meaning of something, the interrogative どういう is used:

⑯ 「立入禁止(たちいりきんし)」は 入(はい)るなと いう 意味(いみ)です。　　'Tachiiri Kinshi' means, 'No Entry'.

⑰ この マークは どういう 意味(いみ)ですか。　　What does this symbol mean?
……洗濯機(せんたくき)で 洗(あら)えると いう 意味(いみ)です。　　…… It means 'machine-washable'.

## 5. S / Plain form } と 言(い)って いました

〜と いいました is used for quoting what someone said (see Lesson 21), while 〜と いって いました is used for reporting what someone said:

⑱ 田中(たなか)さんは「あした 休(やす)みます」と 言(い)って いました。
Mr. Tanaka said, "I'm taking the day off tomorrow".

⑲ 田中(たなか)さんは あした 休(やす)むと 言(い)って いました。
Mr. Tanaka said he would take the day off tomorrow.

## 6. S / Plain form } と 伝(つた)えて いただけませんか

This is used when the speaker is politely asking someone to pass a message on for him or her.

⑳ ワンさんに「あとで 電話(でんわ)を ください」と 伝(つた)えて いただけませんか。
Would you mind asking Mr. Wang to call me later?

㉑ すみませんが、渡辺(わたなべ)さんに あしたの パーティーは 6時(じ)からだと 伝(つた)えて いただけませんか。
I'm sorry to bother you, but would you mind telling Ms. Watanabe that tomorrow's party starts at 6 o'clock?

# Lesson 34

## I. Vocabulary

| | | |
|---|---|---|
| みがきます I<br>［はを～］ | 磨きます<br>［歯を～］ | brush [one's teeth], polish |
| くみたてます II | 組み立てます | assemble |
| おります I | 折ります | bend, fold, break, snap |
| きが つきます I<br>［わすれものに～］ | 気が つきます<br>［忘れ物に～］ | notice, become aware of [things left behind] |
| つけます II<br>［しょうゆを～］ | | put [in soy sauce] |
| みつかります I<br>［かぎが～］ | 見つかります | [a key] be found |
| しつもんします III | 質問します | ask a question |
| さします I<br>［かさを～］ | ［傘を～］ | put up [an umbrella] |
| スポーツクラブ | | sports club |
| ［お］しろ | ［お］城 | castle |
| せつめいしょ | 説明書 | explanatory pamphlet, instruction book |
| ず | 図 | figure, drawing |
| せん | 線 | line |
| やじるし | 矢印 | arrow (sign) |
| くろ | 黒 | black (noun) |
| しろ* | 白 | white (noun) |
| あか* | 赤 | red (noun) |
| あお* | 青 | blue (noun) |
| こん | 紺 | navy blue, dark blue (noun) |
| きいろ* | 黄色 | yellow (noun) |
| ちゃいろ* | 茶色 | brown (noun) |
| しょうゆ | | soya, soy sauce |
| ソース | | sauce, Worcestershire sauce |
| おきゃく［さん］ | お客［さん］ | visitor, guest, customer, client |
| ～か ～ | | ～ or ～ |
| ゆうべ | | last night |
| さっき | | a short while ago |

### 〈会話(かいわ)〉

| | |
|---|---|
| 茶道(さどう) | tea ceremony |
| お茶(ちゃ)を たてますⅡ | make (green) tea (at a tea ceremony) |
| 先(さき)に | first, ahead |
| 載(の)せますⅡ | place on, load onto |
| これで いいですか。 | Is this all right? |
| いかがですか。 | How is it? |
| 苦(にが)い | bitter |

### 〈読(よ)み物(もの)〉

| | |
|---|---|
| 親子(おやこ)どんぶり | a bowl of cooked rice with chicken and egg |
| 材料(ざいりょう) | material, ingredient |
| ～分(ぶん) | portion for ～ (used for indicating quantity) |
| ーグラム | ー gramme |
| ー個(こ) | (counter for small objects) |
| たまねぎ | onion |
| 4分(ぶん)の1 (1/4) | one fourth |
| 調味料(ちょうみりょう) | seasoning, flavouring |
| 適当(てきとう)な 大(おお)きさに | in right size |
| なべ | pan, pot |
| 火(ひ) | fire, heating |
| 火(ひ)に かけますⅡ | put on the stove |
| 煮(に)ますⅡ | cook, boil |
| 煮(に)えますⅡ | be cooked, be boiled |
| どんぶり | bowl |
| たちますⅠ | pass (time) |

## II. Translation

### Sentence Patterns

1. I will write what my teacher told me to.
2. I brush my teeth after eating.
3. I drink coffee without sugar.

### Example Sentences

1. This is the new robot.
   ……What kind of robot is it?
   It copies everything you do.
2. Do you assemble this table yourself?
   ……Yes, please assemble it according to the instructions.
3. Hold on, please. You put the soy sauce in after the sugar, you know.
   ……Oh, I see.
4. Shall we go for a drink after work?
   ……Sorry, today's the day when I go to my sports club.
5. What should I wear when I go to my friend's wedding ceremony?
   ……Well, in Japan, men wear a black or dark-blue suit with a white tie.
6. Do you put sauce on this?
   ……No, please eat it without putting anything on it.
7. I've started using the stairs instead of the lift recently.
   ……Good exercise, isn't it?

### Conversation

**Please do as I did**

Klara: I'd like to see a tea ceremony......
Watanabe: All right, shall we go together next Saturday?

…………………………………………………………

Tea Ceremony Teacher: Please make the tea, Ms. Watanabe.
Please have a cake, Klara.
Klara: Oh, do we eat cake first?
Tea Ceremony Teacher: Yes, the tea tastes much better if you drink it after first eating a sweet cake.
Klara: Oh.
Tea Ceremony Teacher: All right, let's drink the tea.
First, pick up the bowl with your right hand and place it on the palm of your left hand.
Next, turn the bowl twice, and then drink.
Klara: Yes.
Tea Ceremony Teacher: All right, please do as I did.

…………………………………………………………

Klara: Is this right?
Tea Ceremony Teacher: Yes. How is it?
Klara: It's a little bitter, but it's nice.

## III. Useful Words & Information

### 料理(りょうり)　Cooking

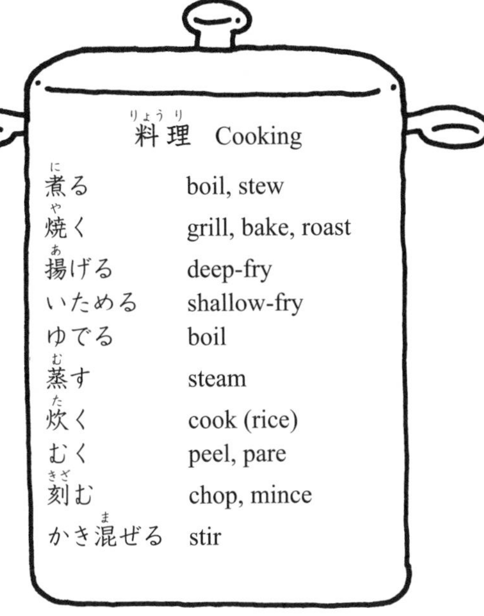

料理(りょうり)　Cooking

| | |
|---|---|
| 煮(に)る | boil, stew |
| 焼(や)く | grill, bake, roast |
| 揚(あ)げる | deep-fry |
| いためる | shallow-fry |
| ゆでる | boil |
| 蒸(む)す | steam |
| 炊(た)く | cook (rice) |
| むく | peel, pare |
| 刻(きざ)む | chop, mince |
| かき混(ま)ぜる | stir |

調味料(ちょうみりょう)　Seasoning

| | |
|---|---|
| しょうゆ | soy sauce |
| 砂糖(さとう) | sugar |
| 塩(しお) | salt |
| 酢(す) | vinegar |
| みそ | miso |
| 油(あぶら) | oil, fat |
| ソース | Worcestershire sauce |
| マヨネーズ | mayonnaise |
| ケチャップ | ketchup |
| からし（マスタード） | mustard |
| こしょう | pepper |
| とうがらし | cayenne pepper |
| しょうが | ginger |
| わさび | Japanese horseradish |
| カレー粉(こ) | curry powder |

台所用品(だいどころようひん)　Cookware and Kitchen Utensils

| | | | |
|---|---|---|---|
| なべ | pot, pan | 炊飯器(すいはんき) | rice cooker |
| やかん | kettle | しゃもじ | rice paddle |
| ふた | lid | 缶切(かんき)り | can opener |
| おたま | ladle | 栓抜(せんぬ)き | bottle opener, corkscrew |
| まな板(いた) | cutting board | ざる | colander, sieve |
| 包丁(ほうちょう) | kitchen knife | ポット | Thermos [flask] |
| ふきん | tea-towel, dishcloth | ガス台(だい) | gas stove |
| フライパン | frying pan | 流(なが)し[台(だい)] | sink |
| 電子(でんし)オーブンレンジ | microwave oven | 換気扇(かんきせん) | ventilation fan |

## IV. Grammar Notes

**1.** 

| $V_1$ た -form<br>N の | とおりに、$V_2$ |
|---|---|

1) $V_1$ た -form とおりに、$V_2$

This indicates doing $V_2$ by the same method or under the same conditions as $V_1$:

① わたしが やった とおりに、やって ください。

Please do it as I did.

② 見た とおりに、話して ください。

Please describe exactly what you saw.

2) N の とおりに、V

This indicates performing an action without deviating from the standard indicated by the preceding phrase:

③ 線の とおりに、紙を 切って ください。

Please cut the paper along the line.

④ 説明書の とおりに、組み立てました。

I assembled it in accordance with the instructions.

[Note] As とおり is a noun, it can be used with an demonstrative such as この, その or あの directly attached, to mean 'by the same method or in the same way as specified by that demonstrative'.

⑤ この とおりに、書いて ください。

Please draw it like this.

**2.** 

| $V_1$ た -form<br>N の | あとで、$V_2$ |
|---|---|

This indicates that the action denoted by $V_2$ happens after the action or situation denoted by $V_1$ or N:

⑥ 新しいのを 買った あとで、なくした 時計が 見つかりました。

After I had bought a new one, the watch I had lost was found.

⑦ 仕事の あとで、飲みに 行きませんか。

Shall we go for a drink after work?

This puts more emphasis on the time context in which the events happen than V て -form から (see Lesson 16), which has the same meaning. Also, unlike with V て -form から, there is no implication that $V_1$ or N is a precondition of, or preparatory action for, $V_2$.

## 3. $V_1$ て -form / $V_1$ ない -form ないで } $V_2$

| $V_1$ て -form | $V_2$ |
|---|---|
| $V_1$ ない -form ないで | |

1) This indicates that $V_1$ is an action or state that accompanies $V_2$. For instance, Examples ⑧ and ⑨ below state whether or not soy sauce is used when the action たべます is performed. $V_1$ and $V_2$ are actions performed by the same person:

⑧ しょうゆを　つけて　食べます。

We eat it with soy sauce.

⑨ しょうゆを　つけないで　食べます。

We eat it without soy sauce.

2) $V_1$ ない -form ないで $V_2$ can also be used to indicate a decision to perform one or other of two mutually-exclusive alternative actions $V_1$ and $V_2$:

⑩ 日曜日は　どこも　行かないで、うちで　ゆっくり　休みます。

I'm not going anywhere on Sunday; I'm going to stay at home and take it easy.

34

# Lesson 35

## I. Vocabulary

| | | |
|---|---|---|
| さきますⅠ | 咲きます | [flowers] bloom |
| [はなが～] | [花が～] | |
| かわりますⅠ | 変わります | [the colour] change |
| [いろが～] | [色が～] | |
| こまりますⅠ | 困ります | be in trouble, have a problem |
| つけますⅡ | 付けます | draw [a circle], mark [with a circle], add |
| [まるを～] | [丸を～] | |
| なおりますⅠ | 治ります、直ります | |
| [びょうきが～] | [病気が～] | recover from [sickness], get well |
| [こしょうが～] | [故障が～] | be fixed, be repaired |
| クリックしますⅢ | | click |
| にゅうりょくしますⅢ | 入力します | input |
| | | |
| ただしい | 正しい | correct, right |
| | | |
| むこう | 向こう | over there, the other side |
| しま | 島 | island |
| みなと | 港 | port, harbour |
| きんじょ | 近所 | neighbourhood, vicinity |
| おくじょう | 屋上 | rooftop |
| かいがい | 海外 | overseas |
| | | |
| やまのぼり | 山登り | mountain climbing |
| | | |
| れきし | 歴史 | history |
| | | |
| きかい | 機会 | chance, opportunity |
| きょか | 許可 | permission |
| まる | 丸 | circle |
| ふりがな | | (kana above or beside kanji indicating its pronunciation) |
| | | |
| せつび | 設備 | equipment, facilities |
| レバー | | lever |
| キー | | key |
| カーテン | | curtain |
| ひも | | string |
| すいはんき | 炊飯器 | rice cooker |
| は | 葉 | leaf |
| | | |
| むかし | 昔 | old days, ancient times |
| | | |
| もっと | | more |
| | | |
| これで おわりましょう。 | これで 終わりましょう。 | Let's finish now. |

| | |
|---|---|
| ※箱根(はこね) | resort and tourist spot in Kanagawa prefecture |
| ※日光(にっこう) | tourist spot in Tochigi prefecture |
| ※アフリカ | Africa |
| ※マンガミュージアム | Kyoto International Manga Museum |
| ※みんなの 学校(がっこう) | a fictitious Japanese language school |
| ※大黒(だいこく)ずし | a fictitious sushi restaurant |
| ※ IMC パソコン 教室(きょうしつ) | a fictitious computer school |
| ※母(はは)の 味(あじ) | a fictitious book |
| ※はる | a fictitious hair salon |
| ※佐藤歯科(さとうしか) | a fictitious dental clinic |
| ※毎日(まいにち)クッキング | a fictitious cooking school |

### 〈会話(かいわ)〉

| | |
|---|---|
| それなら | in that case |
| 夜行(やこう)バス | overnight bus |
| さあ | Well, let me see. (used when unsure of something) |
| 旅行社(りょこうしゃ) | travel agency |
| 詳(くわ)しい | detailed |
| スキー 場(じょう) | ski resort, ski area |
| ※草津(くさつ) | resort in Gunma prefecture |
| ※志賀高原(しがこうげん) | national park in Nagano prefecture |

### 〈読(よ)み物(もの)〉

| | |
|---|---|
| 朱(しゅ) | vermilion |
| 交(まじ)わります I | keep company with |
| ことわざ | proverb |
| 関係(かんけい) | relationship |
| 仲(なか)よく しますⅢ | be on good terms with |
| 必要(ひつよう)[な] | necessary, essential |

## II. Translation

### Sentence Patterns

1. When spring comes, the cherry blossoms bloom.
2. When the weather's fine, you can see an island over there.
3. If you're going on a trip to Hokkaido, June is best.

### Example Sentences

1. I can't open the car window......
   ······It'll open if you press that button.
2. Are there any other opinions?
   ······No, not particularly.
   In that case, let's finish now.
3. How do you like life in Japan?
   ······It's very convenient, but I think it would be better if living costs were a little lower.
4. Does the report have to be in by tomorrow?
   ······If that's too difficult, please hand it in by Friday.
5. I'd like to borrow a book; how do I go about it?
   ······Please ask someone at reception to make you a card.
6. I'm thinking of going away for two or three days; can you recommend anywhere good?
   ······Well, if it's for two or three days, I think Hakone or Nikko would be good.

### Conversation

**Do you know any good places?**

Thawaphon: Mr. Suzuki, I want to go skiing with some friends during the winter holidays; do you know any good places?
Suzuki: How many days are you planning to go for?
Thawaphon: About three.
Suzuki: In that case, I think Kusatsu or Shiga Kogen would be good.
They've got hot springs, too......
Thawaphon: How do you get there?
Suzuki: You can go by JR, but the overnight bus is convenient, because you arrive in the morning.
Thawaphon: I see. Which is cheaper?
Suzuki: Hmm......if you go to a travel agency, you'll be able to find out more of the details.
Thawaphon: And we don't have any ski equipment or clothes, either......
Suzuki: You can hire all of those at the ski area.
If you're concerned about it, you can book them at the travel agency as well......
Thawaphon: I see. Thank you very much.

## III. Useful Words & Information

### ことわざ　Proverbs

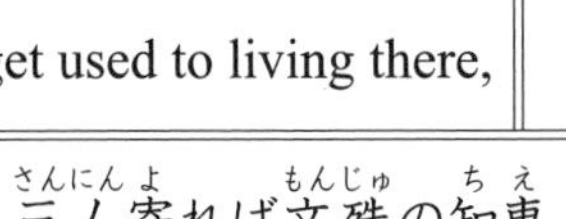

住(す)めば都(みやこ)

*There's no place like home.*

Wherever you live, once you get used to living there, it becomes your home.

三人(さんにん)寄(よ)れば文殊(もんじゅ)の知恵(ちえ)

*Two heads are better than one.*

Even three not especially intelligent people can come up with a good plan if they put their heads together.

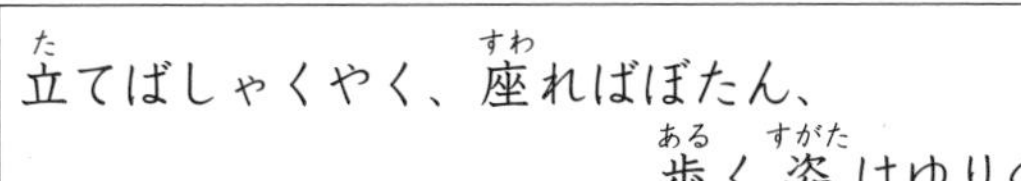

立(た)てばしゃくやく、座(すわ)ればぼたん、歩(ある)く姿(すがた)はゆりの花(はな)

A beautiful woman is like a Chinese peony when standing, a tree peony when sitting, and a lily when walking.

ちりも積(つ)もれば山(やま)となる

*Many a little makes a mickle. (Mighty oaks from tiny acorns grow.)*

Literally 'If enough dust is piled up, it forms a mountain' (even the smallest things turn into something big if enough of them are collected).

うわさをすれば影(かげ)

*Speak of the devil [and he is sure to appear].*

People often appear just as one is talking about them.

苦(く)あれば楽(らく)あり、楽(らく)あれば苦(く)あり

*Life is full of ups and downs. (There's no pleasure without pain.)*

There will be pleasure after suffering, and, conversely, hardship after ease. Life is never either all pain or all pleasure, but a mixture of the two.

## IV. Grammar Notes

### 1. How to create the conditional form (See Exercise A1, Lesson 35, Main Text)

Group I: Change the い -column sound that is the final sound of the ます -form to the え -column sound and add ば .

Group II: Add れば to the ます -form.

Group III: しーます → すれば　　きーます → くれば

[Note] To convert the negative form of a verb (e.g. いかない ) to the conditional form, add なければ to the ない -form (e.g. いか ).

い -adj: Change the い to ければ .

な -adj: Delete the な and add なら .

N: Add なら .

### 2. Conditional form、～

1) Expressing something as a precondition for what is expressed in the following (main) clause to happen:

① ボタンを 押せば、窓が 開きます。　If you press the button, the window will open.

② 彼が 行けば、わたしも 行きます。　If he goes, I'll go too.

③ あした 都合が よければ、来て ください。
If it's convenient for you, please come tomorrow.

④ いい 天気なら、向こうに 島が 見えます。
When the weather's fine, you can see an island over there.

2) Responding to what someone has said or to an explanation of a situation:

⑤ ボールペンが ないんですが。
……ボールペンが なければ、鉛筆で 書いて ください。
I don't have a ballpoint pen.
…… If you don't have a ballpoint pen, please write in pencil.

⑥ あしたまでに レポートを 出さなければ なりませんか。
……無理なら、金曜日までに 出して ください。
Do I have to hand in the report by tomorrow?
…… If that's too difficult, please hand it in by Friday.

As a rule, intentions, hopes, orders , requests, etc. only appear in the following (main) clause, when the subjects of the preceding and following clauses are different (as in Example ② ) or when the predicate of the preceding clause is conditional (as in Examples ③ and ⑤ ).

[For reference] Here is a comparison of the expressions introduced in this lesson with similar expressions introduced in previous lessons:

1) ～と (See Lesson 23)

と indicates that, if the action or state appearing before it occurs, the situation, action, phenomenon or state expressed in the main clause following it will inevitably occur. Intentions, hopes, orders, requests, etc, do not appear in the following (main) clause:

⑦ ここを 押すと、ドアが 開きます。　If you press here, the door will open.

⑦ can also be expressed using ～ば :

⑧ ここを 押せば、ドアが 開きます。　If you press here, the door will open.

2）～たら (See Lesson 25)

～たら has two usages: (1) for showing a hypothetical condition, and (2) indicating that an action or state will occur or appear after certain conditions have been met, when it is known that those conditions will be met. An intention, hope, order, request, etc. can be used in the following (main) clause.

⑨ 東京(とうきょう)へ 来(き)たら、ぜひ 連絡(れんらく)して ください。

Please be sure to contact me when you come to Tokyo.

×東京(とうきょう)へ 来(く)ると、ぜひ 連絡(れんらく)して ください。

×東京(とうきょう)へ 来(く)れば、ぜひ 連絡(れんらく)して ください。

⑩ 田中(たなか)さんが 東京(とうきょう)へ 来(く)れば、[わたしは] 会(あ)いに 行(い)きます。

If you come to Tokyo, Mr. Tanaka, I'll come to meet you.

When the speaker's intention appears in the following (main) clause as in Example ⑨, only ～たら can be used; ～と and ～ば cannot.

However, ～ば can be used in this case when the subjects of the predicate and following (main) clauses are different, as in Example ⑩. Thus, ～たら can be said to have the widest range of uses; but, being a colloquial expression, it is not usually used in writing.

## 3. Interrogative V conditional form いいですか

This is an expression used when asking the listener for advice or instructions. It can be used in the same way as ～たら いいですか, which was introduced in Lesson 26.

⑪ 本(ほん)を 借(か)りたいんですが、どう すれば いいですか。

I'd like to borrow a book; what do I need to do?

⑫ 本(ほん)を 借(か)りたいんですが、どう したら いいですか。

I'd like to borrow a book; what should I do? (See Lesson 26)

## 4. N なら、～

N なら、～ can also be used when giving information to someone about something they have just said:

⑬ 温泉(おんせん)に 行(い)きたいんですが、どこが いいですか。

……温泉(おんせん)なら、白馬(はくば)が いいですよ。

I'd like to go a hot spring; where would be good?

…… If it's a hot spring you're after, Hakuba is good.

## 5. ～は ありませんか (negative question)

⑭ 2、3日(にち) 旅行(りょこう)を しようと 思(おも)って いるんですが、どこか いい 所(ところ)は ありませんか。

I'm thinking of going on holiday for two or three days; do you know of anywhere good?

The いい ところは ありませんか in Example ⑭ means the same as いい ところは ありますか, but it is a more considerate way of asking something because using ありませんか makes it easier for the listener to answer in the negative. In fact, the negative question form is generally a more polite way of asking something. The answer will be either はい、あります or いいえ、ありません.

# Lesson 36

## I. Vocabulary

| | | |
|---|---|---|
| あいますⅠ | | encounter [an accident] |
| ［じこに～］ | ［事故に～］ | |
| ちょきんしますⅢ | 貯金します | save money |
| すぎますⅡ | 過ぎます | pass [7 o'clock] |
| ［7じを～］ | ［7時を～］ | |
| なれますⅡ | 慣れます | get accustomed to [one's job] |
| ［しごとに～］ | ［仕事に～］ | |
| くさりますⅠ | 腐ります | [food] rot |
| ［たべものが～］ | ［食べ物が～］ | |
| けんどう | 剣道 | kendo (Japanese style fencing) |
| じゅうどう* | 柔道 | judo |
| ラッシュ | | rush hour |
| うちゅう | 宇宙 | space, universe |
| きょく | 曲 | a piece of music |
| まいしゅう | 毎週 | every week |
| まいつき* | 毎月 | every month |
| まいとし* | 毎年 | every year |
| （まいねん） | | |
| このごろ | | these days |
| やっと | | finally |
| かなり | | fairly |
| かならず | 必ず | without fail, by any means |
| ぜったいに | 絶対に | absolutely |
| じょうずに | 上手に | well, skillfully |
| できるだけ | | as much as possible |
| ほとんど | | almost all (in affirmative sentences), hardly, scarcely (in negative sentences) |
| ※ショパン | | Chopin, Polish musician (1810-49) |

## 〈会話(かいわ)〉

| | |
|---|---|
| お客様(きゃくさま) | visitor, guest, customer, client (respectful equivalent of おきゃくさん) |
| 特別(とくべつ)[な] | special |
| して いらっしゃいます | be doing (respectful equivalent of して います) |
| 水泳(すいえい) | swimming |
| 違(ちが)います I | be different |
| 使(つか)って いらっしゃるんですね。 | You're using, aren't you? (respectful equivalent of つかって いるんですね) |
| チャレンジしますⅢ | challenge |
| 気持(きも)ち | spirit, mood |

## 〈読(よ)み物(もの)〉

| | |
|---|---|
| 乗(の)り物(もの) | vehicle, means of transportation |
| ー世紀(せいき) | -th century |
| 遠(とお)く | far, remote place |
| 珍(めずら)しい | rare, uncommon |
| 汽車(きしゃ) | locomotive |
| 汽船(きせん) | steam boat |
| 大勢(おおぜい)の ～ | many (people) |
| 運(はこ)びます I | carry, transport |
| 利用(りよう)しますⅢ | use |
| 自由(じゆう)に | freely |

## II. Translation

### Sentence Patterns

1. I practise every day in order to become able to swim fast.
2. I finally learnt to ride a bicycle.
3. I try to write something in my diary every day.

### Example Sentences

1. Is that an electronic dictionary?
   ……Yes. I have it so that I can check it right away when I come across a word I don't know.
2. What do the red circles on your calendar mean?
   ……They show rubbish collection days. They're there so I don't forget.
3. Have you already got used to Japanese food?
   ……Yes. I couldn't eat it at first, but now I can eat anything.
4. Have you learnt how to play any Chopin pieces?
   ……No, I can't play any yet.
   I'd like to learn to play some soon.
5. The new road is finished, isn't it?
   ……Yes. We can get back to my husband's home town in four hours now.
6. Don't you eat anything sweet?
   ……No, I do my best not to.
7. The examination starts at nine o'clock. Please make sure you're not late.
   If you're late, you won't be allowed in.
   ……Yes, OK.





### Conversation

**I try to take some exercise every day**

Announcer: Hello everyone. Our guest today is Yone Ogawa, who is eighty years old this year.

Yone Ogawa: Hello.

Announcer: You're very fit, aren't you? Are you doing something special?

Yone Ogawa: I try to take some exercise every day.

Announcer: What kind of exercise?

Yone Ogawa: Dancing, swimming, and so on......
I've recently become able to swim five hundred metres.

Announcer: That's amazing. How about your diet?

Yone Ogawa: I eat anything, but I'm particularly fond of fish.
I try to cook something different every day.

Announcer: You make good use of your mind and body, don't you?

Yone Ogawa: Yes. I want to go to France next year, so I've started studying French, too.

Announcer: It's important to be prepared to give anything a go, isn't it?
It's been great talking with you. Thank you very much.

## III. Useful Words & Information

### 健康　Health

いいださん

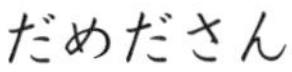

だめださん

**いいださん**

- 規則正しい生活をする
  lead a well-regulated life
- 早寝、早起きをする
  keep early hours
- 運動する／スポーツをする
  take exercise/do sports
- よく歩く
  walk a lot
- 好き嫌いがない
  have no particular likes and dislikes
- 栄養のバランスを考えて食べる
  have a balanced diet
- 健康診断を受ける
  have health checks

**だめださん**

- 夜更かしをする
  stay up late
- あまり運動しない
  take little exercise
- 好き嫌いがある
  have many likes and dislikes
- よくインスタント食品を食べる
  often eat instant foods
- 外食が多い
  often eat out
- たばこを吸う
  smoke
- よくお酒を飲む
  drink a lot

### 5つの大切な栄養素とそれを含む食べ物
Five Important Nutriments and Foods Containing Them

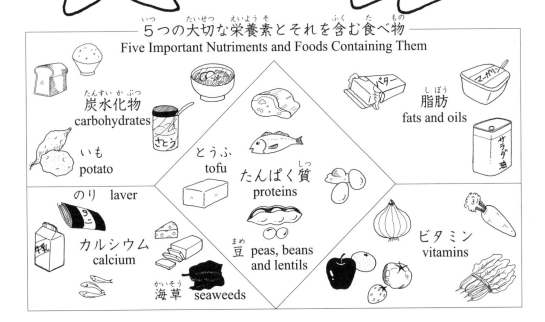

炭水化物
carbohydrates

いも
potato

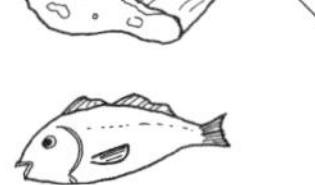

脂肪
fats and oils

とうふ
tofu

たんぱく質
proteins

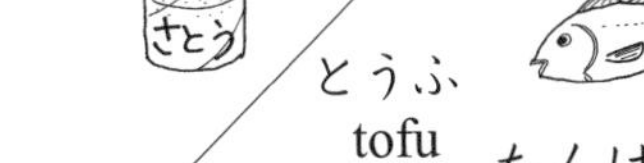

のり　laver

カルシウム
calcium

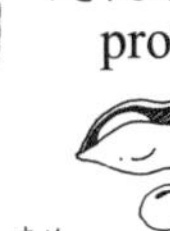

豆　peas, beans and lentils

海草　seaweeds

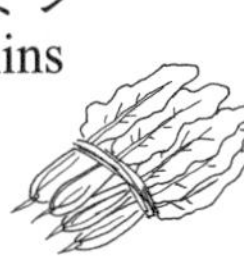

ビタミン
vitamins

## IV. Grammar Notes

**1.**

| $V_1$ dictionary form<br>$V_1$ ない-form ない | ように、$V_2$ |
|---|---|

This usage indicates taking the action denoted by $V_2$ in order to achieve the situation expressed by ～ように. The dictionary form of a non-volitional verb (such as a potential verb, わかります, みえます, きこえます, なります, etc., as in Example ①) or a verb's negative form (as in Example ②) is used before ように:

① 速く 泳げるように、毎日 練習して います。

I'm practising every day so I can become able to swim fast.

② 忘れないように、メモして ください。

Please note it down so you don't forget it.

**2.** **V dictionary form ように なります**

1) なります indicates a change of state. When a potential verb, or verbs such as わかります and みえます are used, V dictionary form ように なります indicates changing from a state of being unable to do something to a state of being able to do it:

③ 毎日 練習すれば、泳げるように なります。

You will learn to swim if you practise every day.

④ やっと 自転車に 乗れるように なりました。

I've finally become able to ride a bicycle.

2) When using いいえ to answer the question ～ように なりましたか in the negative, the answer is given as follows:

⑤ ショパンの 曲が 弾けるように なりましたか。
……いいえ、まだ 弾けません。

Have you learnt to play any Chopin pieces?
…… No, I can't play any yet.

[Note] Although not introduced in the Main Text, when a verb other than a potential verb, わかります or みえます appears in Sentence Pattern 2., it means that a practice that previously did not exist has come into being, as in Example ⑥:

⑥ 日本人は 100年ぐらいまえから 牛肉や 豚肉を 食べるように なりました。

The Japanese started to eat beef and pork about a hundred years ago.

**3.**

| V dictionary form<br>V ない-form ない | ように します |
|---|---|

1) ～ように して います

This indicates that the speaker tries to perform a certain behaviour habitually:

⑦ 毎日 運動して、何でも 食べるように して います。

I try to exercise every day and eat a wide range of foods.

⑧ 歯に 悪いですから、甘い 物を 食べないように して います。

I try not to eat sweet things because they're bad for the teeth.

2) ～ように して ください

This expression is used to ask someone to try to acquire the habit of performing a certain behaviour. While ～て／～ないで ください is a direct expression of a request, ～ように して ください is an indirect expression of a request and is therefore more polite. It is used in the following ways:

⑨ もっと 野菜(やさい)を 食(た)べるように して ください。

Please try to eat more vegetables.

⑩ 絶対(ぜったい)に パスポートを なくさないように して ください。

Please be sure not to lose your passport.

[Note] ～ように して ください cannot be used to make a request for an action to be performed on the spot:

⑪ すみませんが、塩(しお)を 取(と)って ください。

Excuse me, please pass the salt.

×すみませんが、塩(しお)を 取(と)るように して ください。

**4.** 早(はや)い→早(はや)く　　上手(じょうず)な→上手(じょうず)に

When an adjective modifies another adjective or a verb, it is used in the ～く form if it is an い-adjective and the ～に form if it is a な-adjective.

⑫ 早(はや)く 上手(じょうず)に お茶(ちゃ)が たてられるように なりたいです。

I want to learn quickly to become good at the tea ceremony.

# Lesson 37

## I. Vocabulary

| | | |
|---|---|---|
| ほめますⅡ | 褒めます | praise |
| しかりますⅠ | | scold |
| さそいますⅠ | 誘います | invite, ask someone to join |
| しょうたいしますⅢ | 招待します | invite |
| たのみますⅠ | 頼みます | ask, request |
| ちゅういしますⅢ | 注意します | warn, advise |
| とりますⅠ | | rob, steal |
| ふみますⅠ | 踏みます | step on |
| こわしますⅠ | 壊します | break, destroy |
| よごしますⅠ | 汚します | make ～ dirty |
| おこないますⅠ | 行います | hold, carry out, practise |
| ゆしゅつしますⅢ | 輸出します | export |
| ゆにゅうしますⅢ | 輸入します | import |
| ほんやくしますⅢ | 翻訳します | translate |
| はつめいしますⅢ | 発明します | invent |
| はっけんしますⅢ | 発見します | discover |
| こめ* | 米 | rice |
| むぎ | 麦 | barley, wheat |
| せきゆ | 石油 | oil |
| げんりょう | 原料 | raw material |
| インスタントラーメン | | instant noodles |
| デート | | date |
| どろぼう | 泥棒 | thief, robber |
| けいかん | 警官 | policeman |
| せかいじゅう | 世界中 | all over the world |
| ～じゅう | ～中 | all over ～ |
| －せいき | －世紀 | -th century |
| なにご | 何語 | what language |
| だれか | | somebody |
| よかったですね。 | | Sounds good. |
| ※オリンピック | | Olympic Games |
| ※ワールドカップ | | World Cup |
| ※東大寺（とうだいじ） | | Todaiji Temple |
| ※大仏（だいぶつ） | | Great Buddha |
| ※江戸時代（えどじだい） | | Edo Period（1603-1868） |
| ※ポルトガル | | Portugal |
| ※サウジアラビア | | Saudi Arabia |

| | |
|---|---|
| ※ロシア | Russia |

**〈会話（かいわ）〉**

| | |
|---|---|
| 皆様（みなさま） | Ladies and gentlemen, everybody (respect equivalent of みなさん) |
| 焼（や）けますⅡ ［うちが～］ | [house] burn down |
| その後（ご） | after that, later |
| 世界遺産（せかいいさん） | World Heritage Site |
| ～の 一（ひと）つ | one of the ～ |
| 金色（きんいろ） | golden colour |
| 本物（ほんもの） | real thing |
| 金（きん） | gold |
| －キロ | － kilogrammes, － kilometres |
| 美（うつく）しい | beautiful, pretty |

**〈読（よ）み物（もの）〉**

| | |
|---|---|
| 豪華（ごうか）［な］ | gorgeous |
| 彫刻（ちょうこく） | engraving, carving, sculpture |
| 言（い）い伝（つた）え | tradition, legend |
| 眠（ねむ）りますⅠ | sleep |
| 彫（ほ）りますⅠ | engrave, carve |
| 仲間（なかま） | colleague, friend |
| しかし | however, but |
| その あと | after that |
| 一生懸命（いっしょうけんめい） | with all one's effort |
| ねずみ | mouse |
| 一匹（いっぴき）も いません。 | There is not a single (mouse). |
| ※東照宮（とうしょうぐう） | shrine dedicated to Tokugawa Ieyasu in Nikko, Tochigi prefecture |
| ※眠（ねむ）り猫（ねこ） | The Sleeping Cat |
| ※左甚五郎（ひだりじんごろう） | famous Japanese sculptor of the Edo Period (1594-1651) |

## II. Translation

### Sentence Patterns

1. When I was a child, I was often scolded by my mother.
2. I had my foot trodden on in a rush-hour train.
3. Horyuji was built in 607.

### Example Sentences

1. I was called in by the department manager this morning.
   ……Had something happened?
   He cautioned me about the way I had written the report of my business trip.
2. What's the matter?
   ……Somebody has taken my umbrella by mistake.
3. Another new star has been discovered.
   ……Has it?
4. Where are they holding this year's World Children's Conference?
   ……In Hiroshima.
5. Beer is made from wheat. This is the wheat used as the raw material.
   ……This turns into beer, right?
6. What language is used in Brazil?
   ……Portuguese [is used].



### Conversation



**Kinkakuji was built in the 14th century**

Guide: Look, everyone. That's the famous Golden Pavilion over there.
It was built in the 14th century.
It burnt down in 1950, but was later rebuilt, and it became a World Heritage site in 1994. It's one of the most popular temples in Kyoto.

Karina: It's beautiful, isn't it? The walls are a golden colour; is that real gold?

Guide: Yes. About twenty kilogrammes of gold were used.

Karina: Really? Is it possible to go inside?

Guide: No, you can't go in.
Please look at it while walking round the pond.

……………………………………………………

Karina: The maple leaves are beautiful, aren't they?

Guide: Yes. Kinkakuji is said to be particularly beautiful in the seasons when the leaves turn red and when snow falls.

## III. Useful Words & Information

### 事故(じこ)・事件(じけん)　Accidents and Incidents

## IV. Grammar Notes

### 1. Passive verbs

| | | Passive verbs | |
|---|---|---|---|
| | | Polite form | Plain form |
| I | かきます | かかれます | かかれる |
| II | ほめます | ほめられます | ほめられる |
| III | きます | こられます | こられる |
| | します | されます | される |

(See Exercise A1, Lesson 37, Main Text)

Passive verbs are conjugated as Group II verbs.
Examples: かかれます　　かかれる　　かかれ(ない)　　かかれて

### 2. $N_1$(person $_1$)は $N_2$(person $_2$)に passive V

This sentence pattern expresses an action performed by person $_2$ in relation to person $_1$ from the standpoint of the person at whom the action is directed (i.e. person $_1$).
Person $_1$ is taken as the topic, and the person taking the action (person $_2$) is indicated by attaching the particle に:

先生が わたしを 褒めました。　　My teacher praised me.

① わたしは 先生に 褒められました。　　I was praised by my teacher.

母が わたしに 買い物を 頼みました。　　My mother asked me to go shopping.

② わたしは 母に 買い物を 頼まれました。
I was asked to go shopping by my mother.

The agent may also be something that moves other than a person (e.g. an animal or vehicle):

③ わたしは 犬に かまれました。　　I was bitten by a dog.

### 3. $N_1$(person $_1$)は $N_2$(person $_2$)に $N_3$を passive V

This expresses person $_2$ performing an action on a possession of, or other thing associated with, person $_1$ (this thing being $N_3$), where, in most cases, person $_1$ regards that action as an inconvenience or annoyance:

弟が わたしの パソコンを 壊しました。
My younger brother broke my PC.

④ わたしは 弟に パソコンを 壊されました。
I had my PC broken by my younger brother.

The agent may also be something that moves other than a person (e.g. an animal or vehicle):

⑤ わたしは 犬に 手を かまれました。
I had my hand bitten by a dog.

[Note 1] It is not the possession that is introduced as the topic but the person who regards the action as an inconvenience or annoyance (the owner). Example ④, for instance, is not framed as わたしの パソコンは おとうとに こわされました.

[Note 2] Since in most cases this sentence pattern indicates that the person subject to the action regards it as an inconvenience or annoyance, care must be taken when using it. When talking about something someone has done for you and for which you feel grateful, you should use ～て もらいます：

×わたしは 友達に 自転車を 修理されました。

⑥ わたしは 友達に 自転車を 修理して もらいました。

My friend repaired my bicycle for me.

## 4. N (tangible/intangible) が／は passive V

A passive verb can be used when it is not necessary to mention who is carrying out the action involved, and the subject or topic can be either tangible or intangible:

⑦ 大阪で 展覧会が 開かれました。

An exhibition was held in Osaka.

⑧ 電話は 19世紀に 発明されました。

The telephone was invented in the 19th century.

⑨ この 本は 世界中で 読まれて います。

This book is read all over the world.

## 5. Nから／Nで つくります

から is used when saying what something is made from, and で is used when saying what something is made of:

⑩ ビールは 麦から 造られます。 Beer is made from barley.

⑪ 昔 日本の 家は 木で 造られました。

Japanese houses used to be built of wood.

## 6. $N_1$の $N_2$

⑫ ビールは 麦から 造られます。 Beer is made from barley.

これが 原料の 麦です。 This is the barley [used as the] raw material.

The construction げんりょうの むぎ in Example ⑫ indicates that the barley mentioned is used as the raw material. Two other examples are ペットの いぬ (Lesson 39) and むすこの ハンス (Lesson 43).

## 7. この／その／あの N (position)

When an demonstrative such as この, その or あの is attached to a noun indicating position, such as うえ, した, なか, となり or ちかく, it indicates where the speaker or listener is in relation to what the positional noun indicates:

⑬ あの 中に 入れますか。 Can you go in there?

The あの なか in Example ⑬ means あの たてものの なか.

# Lesson 38

## I. Vocabulary

| | | |
|---|---|---|
| さんかしますⅢ<br>［りょこうに～］ | 参加します<br>［旅行に～］ | join [a tour], participate, attend |
| そだてますⅡ | 育てます | breed, bring up |
| はこびますⅠ | 運びます | carry, transport |
| にゅういんしますⅢ | 入院します | enter hospital |
| たいいんしますⅢ | 退院します | leave hospital |
| いれますⅡ*<br>［でんげんを～］ | 入れます<br>［電源を～］ | turn on [the power switch] |
| きりますⅠ<br>［でんげんを～］ | 切ります<br>［電源を～］ | turn off [the power switch] |
| かけますⅡ<br>［かぎを～］ | 掛けます | lock |
| つきますⅠ<br>［うそを～］ | | tell [a lie] |
| きもちが いい | 気持ちが いい | pleasant, agreeable |
| きもちが わるい* | 気持ちが 悪い | unpleasant, disgusting |
| おおきな ～ | 大きな ～ | large ～, big ～ |
| ちいさな ～ | 小さな ～ | small ～, little ～ |
| あかちゃん | 赤ちゃん | baby |
| しょうがっこう | 小学校 | elementary school |
| ちゅうがっこう* | 中学校 | junior high school |
| えきまえ | 駅前 | the area in front of the station |
| かいがん | 海岸 | seaside, seashore |
| こうじょう | 工場 | factory |
| むら | 村 | village |
| かな | | hiragana and katakana script |
| ゆびわ | 指輪 | ring |
| でんげん | 電源 | power switch |
| しゅうかん | 習慣 | habit |
| けんこう | 健康 | health |
| ～せい | ～製 | made in ～ |
| おととし | | the year before last |
| ［あ、］いけない。 | | Oops!/Oh, no! (used when one has made a mistake) |



38

| | |
|---|---|
| おさきに［しつれいします］。　お先に［失礼します］。 | Excuse me (for leaving before you). |
| ※原爆(げんばく)ドーム | dome commemorating the atomic bombing of Hiroshima |
| ※出雲大社(いずもたいしゃ) | a shrine in Izumo city in Shimane prefecture |
| ※チェンマイ | Chiangmai (in Thailand) |

**〈会話(かいわ)〉**

| | |
|---|---|
| 回覧(かいらん) | circular |
| 研究室(けんきゅうしつ) | study room, professor's office, laboratory |
| きちんと | neatly, tidily |
| 整理(せいり)しますⅢ | sort (things) out |
| 方法(ほうほう) | method |
| ～と いう | entitled ～, named ～, called ～ |
| －冊(さつ) | (counter for books, etc.) |
| はんこ | seal, stamp |
| 押(お)しますⅠ ［はんこを～］ | affix [a seal], stamp |

**〈読み物(よみもの)〉**

| | |
|---|---|
| 双子(ふたご) | twins |
| 姉妹(しまい) | sisters |
| 5年生(ねんせい) | fifth grade, fifth year |
| 似(に)て いますⅡ | resemble, be like |
| 性格(せいかく) | character |
| おとなしい | quiet, gentle |
| 優(やさ)しい | kind, gentle, tender-hearted |
| 世話(せわ)を しますⅢ | take care of |
| 時間(じかん)が たちますⅠ | time passes by |
| 大好(だいす)き［な］ | like very much |
| －点(てん) | － points |
| 気(き)が 強(つよ)い | tough, strong-willed |
| けんかしますⅢ | quarrel, fight |
| 不思議(ふしぎ)［な］ | mysterious, strange |
| 年齢(ねんれい) | age |
| しかた | way (of doing something) |

## II. Translation

### Sentence Patterns

1. Painting pictures is fun.
2. I like looking at the stars.
3. I forgot to bring my wallet.
4. It was last March that I came to Japan.

### Example Sentences

1. Are you still keeping a diary?
   ······No, I gave up after three days.
   It's easy to start, but difficult to carry on, isn't it?
2. What a lovely garden!
   ······Thank you very much.
   My husband is very good at growing flowers.
3. How is Tokyo?
   ······There are so many people, aren't there, and everyone walks very fast, don't they?
4. Oh, no!
   ······What's wrong?
   I forgot to shut the car window.
5. Did you know that Ms. Miyazaki has had a baby?
   ······No, I didn't. When was it?
   About a month ago.
6. Do you remember the person you first fell in love with?
   ······Yes. I first met her in a classroom at primary school.
   She was my music teacher.





### Conversation

**I like putting things in order**

University Staff Member: Professor Watt, here's the circular.
Watt: Ah, thank you. Please leave it there.
University Staff Member: Your office is always tidy, isn't it?
Watt: Yes, I like putting things in order.
University Staff Member: The books are neatly lined up, too......
You're good at organising, aren't you?
Watt: I once wrote a book entitled 'How to Organise Effectively'.
University Staff Member: Really? That's amazing.
Watt: It didn't sell very well, though.
Would you like me to bring you a copy?

··························································

University Staff Member: Good morning.
Watt: Oh, I forgot to bring the book. Sorry.
University Staff Member: Never mind. But please don't forget to stamp the circulars.
Last month's wasn't stamped either, you know.

## III. Useful Words & Information

### 位置（いち） Location

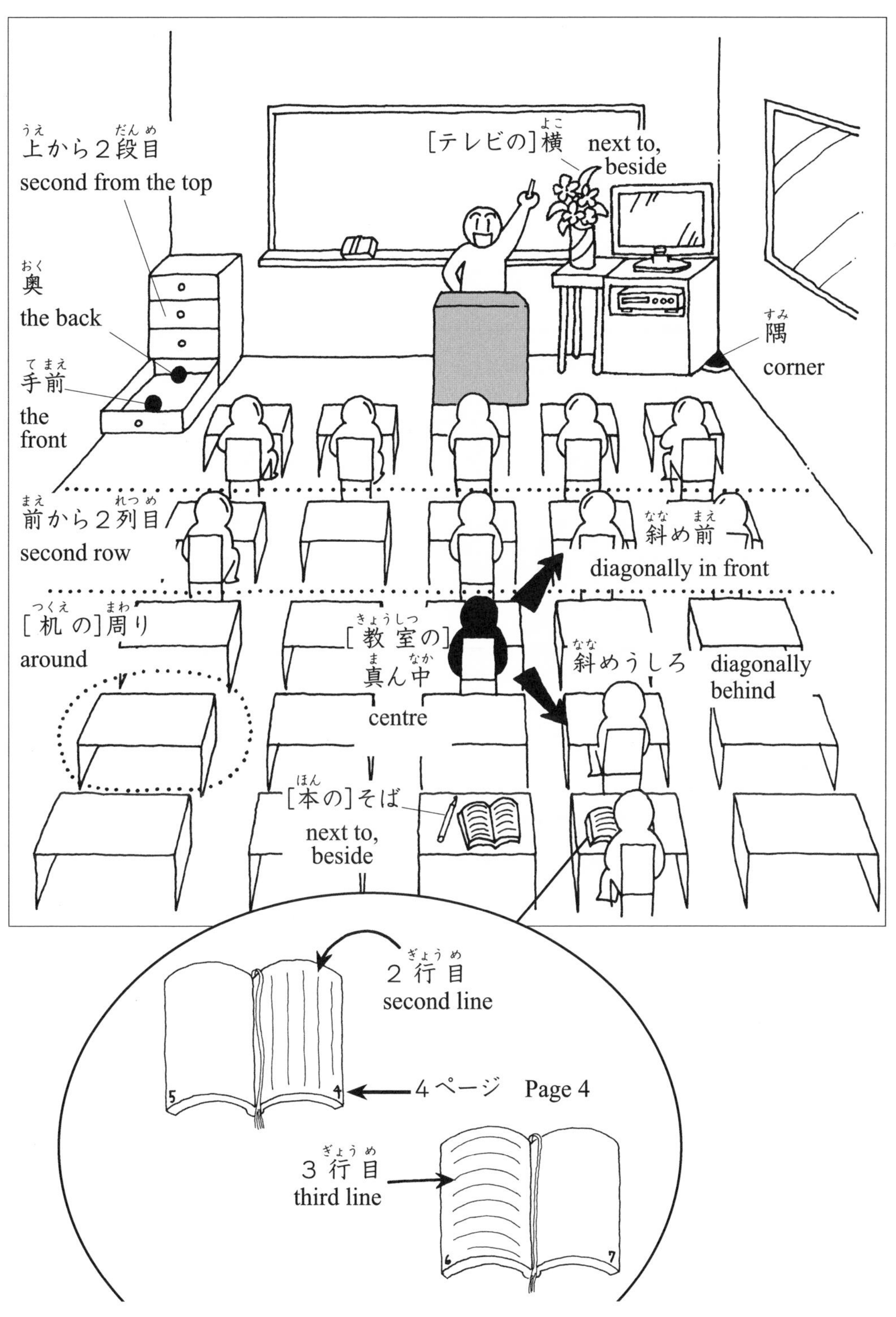




38

# IV. Grammar Notes

## 1. の as a nominaliser

の has the function of nominalising various expressions. The verbs, adjectives and nouns to which の is attached take the plain form, not the polite form. Nominalised expressions can form various elements of sentences, as illustrated below.

## 2. V dictionary form のは adj です

① テニスは おもしろいです。 Tennis is fun.

② テニスを するのは おもしろいです。 Playing tennis is fun.

③ テニスを 見(み)るのは おもしろいです。 Watching tennis is fun.

This is a sentence pattern in which V dictionary form の is presented as the topic by attaching は to it. Adjectives such as むずかしい, やさしい, おもしろい, たのしい and たいへん[な] are often used in this sentence pattern.

Compared with a sentence such as ①, which does not employ の and which merely states that 'tennis' in general is fun, Examples ② and ③ are more precise, stating that the specific acts of 'playing' tennis and 'watching' tennis are fun.

## 3. V dictionary form のが adj です

④ わたしは 花(はな)が 好(す)きです。 I like flowers.

⑤ わたしは 花(はな)を 育(そだ)てるのが 好(す)きです。 I like growing flowers.

⑥ 東京(とうきょう)の 人(ひと)は 歩(ある)くのが 速(はや)いです。 Tokyo people walk fast.

In these examples, 'V dictionary form の' is what is described by the adjective. Adjectives describing things like preferences, skills and abilities, such as すき[な], きらい[な], じょうず[な], へた[な], はやい and おそい, are often seen in this sentence pattern.

## 4. V dictionary form のを 忘(わす)れました forgot to do ～

⑦ かぎを 忘(わす)れました。 I forgot my key.

⑧ 牛乳(ぎゅうにゅう)を 買(か)うのを 忘(わす)れました。 I forgot to buy some milk.

⑨ 車(くるま)の 窓(まど)を 閉(し)めるのを 忘(わす)れました。 I forgot to shut the car window.

These are examples in which 'V dictionary form の' has become an object, marked by を. They introduce an action that was supposed to have been taken regarding the object, and state that it has been forgotten.

## 5. V plain form のを 知(し)って いますか　Do you know that ～?

This is an example in which 'V plain form の' has become an object, marked by を. It is used when asking whether someone knows something specific:

⑩ 鈴木(すずき)さんが 来月(らいげつ) 結婚(けっこん)するのを 知(し)って いますか。

Did you know that Mr. Suzuki is getting married next month?

[Note] The difference between しりません and しりませんでした:

⑪ 木村(きむら)さんに 赤(あか)ちゃんが 生(う)まれたのを 知(し)って いますか。

……いいえ、知(し)りませんでした。

Did you know that Ms. Kimura has had a baby?

…… No, I didn't.

⑫ ミラーさんの 住所(じゅうしょ)を 知(し)って いますか。　Do you know Mr. Miller's address?

……いいえ、知(し)りません。　…… No, I don't.

In Example ⑪, the listener replies, しりませんでした because he or she did not possess the information that Ms. Kimura had had a baby until asked the question, but came into possession of that information through being asked the question. In Example ⑫, on the other hand, the listener possesses the information neither before the question nor after it, and therefore replies, しりません.

## 6.

| | | |
|---|---|---|
| **V**<br>**い-adj** | **plain form** | のは $N_2$ です |
| **な-adj**<br>$N_1$ | **plain form**<br>～だ→～な | |

This sentence pattern is a way of emphasising $N_2$:

⑬ 初(はじ)めて 会(あ)ったのは いつですか。　When was it that we first met?

……3年(ねん)まえです。　…… It was three years ago.

In Example ⑬, the speaker stresses that what he or she wants to ask about, in regard to his or her first meeting with the listener, is specifically <u>when</u> it took place.

This sentence pattern is often used to correct what someone has said, as in Example ⑭.

⑭ バンコクで 生(う)まれたんですか。

……いいえ、生(う)まれたのは チェンマイです。

Were you born in Bangkok?

…… No, I was born in Chiang Mai.

The subject of the sentence prior to ～のは is indicated by が, not by は:

⑮ 父(ちち)が 生(う)まれたのは 北海道(ほっかいどう)の 小(ち)さな 村(むら)です。

My father was born in a small village in Hokkaido.

# Lesson 39

## I. Vocabulary

| | | |
|---|---|---|
| こたえますⅡ<br>［しつもんに～］ | 答えます<br>［質問に～］ | answer [a question] |
| たおれますⅡ<br>［ビルが～］ | 倒れます | [a building] fall down |
| とおりますⅠ<br>［みちを～］ | 通ります<br>［道を～］ | pass [along a street] |
| しにますⅠ | 死にます | die |
| びっくりしますⅢ | | be surprised |
| がっかりしますⅢ | | be disappointed |
| あんしんしますⅢ | 安心します | be relieved |
| けんかしますⅢ | | quarrel, fight |
| りこんしますⅢ | 離婚します | divorce |
| ふとりますⅠ | 太ります | get fat, gain weight |
| やせますⅡ* | | get slim, lose weight |
| ふくざつ［な］ | 複雑［な］ | complicated, complex |
| じゃま［な］ | 邪魔［な］ | obstructive, in the way |
| かたい | 硬い | hard, tough, solid |
| やわらかい* | 軟らかい | soft, tender |
| きたない | 汚い | dirty |
| うれしい | | glad, happy |
| かなしい | 悲しい | sad |
| はずかしい | 恥ずかしい | embarrassed, ashamed |
| しゅしょう | 首相 | Prime Minister |
| じしん | 地震 | earthquake |
| つなみ | 津波 | tsunami, tidal wave |
| たいふう | 台風 | typhoon |
| かみなり | 雷 | thunder |
| かじ | 火事 | fire |
| じこ | 事故 | accident |
| ハイキング | | hiking |
| ［お］みあい | ［お］見合い | a meeting arranged with a view to marriage |
| そうさ | 操作 | operation（～します：operate） |
| かいじょう | 会場 | venue, event location |
| ～だい | ～代 | charge, fare, fee |
| ～や | ～屋 | -er (e.g. baker, grocer, etc.) |
| フロント | | front desk, reception desk |
| ーごうしつ | ー号室 | room number ー |

| | | |
|---|---|---|
| タオル | | towel |
| せっけん | | soap |
| おおぜい | 大勢 | a great number (of people) |
| おつかれさまでした。 | お疲れさまでした。 | Thank you for your hard work. (used to express appreciation for a colleague's or subordinate's work) |
| うかがいます。 | 伺います。 | I'm coming. (humble equivalent of いきます) |

**〈会話〉**

| | |
|---|---|
| 途中で | on the way, in the midst of |
| トラック | truck, lorry |
| ぶつかりますⅠ | bump, collide |

**〈読み物〉**

| | |
|---|---|
| 大人 | adult |
| しかし | however, but |
| また | and |
| 洋服 | Western clothes |
| 西洋化しますⅢ | be Westernized |
| 合いますⅠ | fit, suit |
| 今では | now |
| 成人式 | coming-of-age celebration |
| 伝統的[な] | traditional |

## II. Translation

### Sentence Patterns

1. I was surprised to hear the news.
2. The building collapsed in an earthquake.
3. I'm not feeling very well, so I'm going to hospital.

### Example Sentences

1. How was your omiai?
   ……I thought he looked very nice in his photograph, but I was disappointed when I met him.
2. We're all going hiking next Saturday; would you like to come?
   ……I'm sorry, I'm afraid I can't come on Saturday. [It's not convenient.]
3. How was yesterday's film?
   ……The story was complicated, and I didn't understand it very well.
4. Sorry I'm late.
   ……What happened?
   The bus was late because of an accident.
5. Shall we go for a quick drink?
   ……Sorry, there's something I have to do. I have to leave now (lit. Excuse me for leaving before you.)
   OK, see you then.
6. I've been sleeping on a futon recently. Handy, aren't they?
   ……What did you do with your bed?
   My room is small, and it was in the way, so I gave it to a friend.



### Conversation



**Sorry I'm late**

| | |
|---|---|
| Miller: | Sorry I'm late, Ms. Nakamura. |
| Section Manager Nakamura: | What happened, Mr. Miller? |
| Miller: | Actually there was an accident on the way, and the bus was late. |
| Section Manager Nakamura: | Was the bus in an accident? |
| Miller: | No, a truck and a car collided at a crossroads, and the bus was stuck. |
| Section Manager Nakamura: | That's too bad.<br>Everyone was worried, because we hadn't heard from you. |
| Miller: | I wanted to call, but I'd left my mobile at home...... I'm very sorry. |
| Section Manager Nakamura: | I understand.<br>Well, let's start the meeting. |

# III. Useful Words & Information

## 気(き)持(も)ち　Feelings

⑧ 地震で ビルが 倒れました。　The building fell down in an earthquake.

⑨ 病気で 会社を 休みました。　I got ill and took some time off work.

## III. Useful Words & Information

### 気持ち（きもち） Feelings

| | | | |
|---|---|---|---|
| うれしい<br>happy | 楽（たの）しい<br>pleasant, enjoyable | 寂（さび）しい<br>lonely | 悲（かな）しい<br>sad |
| おもしろい<br>amusing, interesting | うらやましい<br>envious | 恥（は）ずかしい<br>embarrassed, ashamed | 懐（なつ）かしい<br>dear, longed for |
| びっくりする<br>be surprised | がっかりする<br>be disappointed | うっとりする<br>be enchanted |  |
| いらいらする<br>be irritated | どきどきする<br>[heart] beat fast, get butterflies in the stomach | はらはらする<br>be in suspense, be on tenterhooks | わくわくする<br>be excited |

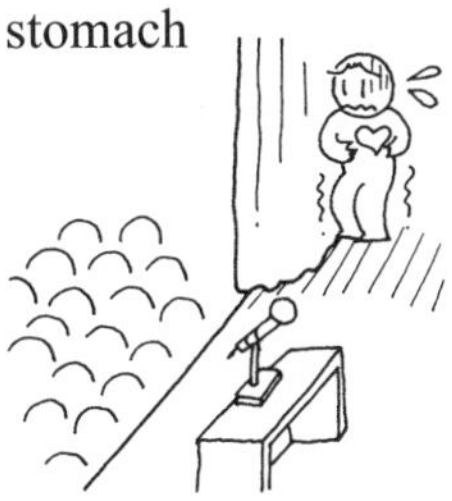

## IV. Grammar Notes

### 1. ～て（で）、～

The sentence pattern ～て（で）、～ was introduced in Lessons 16 and 34, but the present lesson introduces the usage in which the first part of the sentence (i.e. the ～て（で） part) indicates a cause or reason for the result indicated in the second part. The second part of the sentence can only be a non-volitional expression or expression of state.

1）

| | |
|---|---|
| V て -form<br>V ない -form なくて<br>い -adj（～~~い~~）→～くて<br>な -adj［~~な~~］→で | 、～ |

The second part of the sentence usually consists of an expression of the following type:

（1）Verbs and adjectives expressing emotions: びっくりします, あんしんします, こまります, さびしい, うれしい, ざんねん［な］, etc:

① ニュースを 聞(き)いて、びっくりしました。
I was surprised to hear the news.

② 家族(かぞく)に 会(あ)えなくて、寂(さび)しいです。
I'm sad at being unable to see my family.

（2）Verbs and expressions expressing potential or state:

③ 土曜日(どようび)は 都合(つごう)が 悪(わる)くて、行(い)けません。
Saturday's no good for me; I can't go.

④ 話(はなし)が 複雑(ふくざつ)で、よく わかりませんでした。
What was being talked about was complicated; I couldn't really follow it.

⑤ 事故(じこ)が あって、バスが 遅(おく)れて しまいました。
There was an accident, and the bus was late.

⑥ 授業(じゅぎょう)に 遅(おく)れて、先生(せんせい)に しかられました。
I was late to the lesson, and the teacher told me off.

［Note］When second part of the sentence consists of an expression embodying intention (an intention, order, invitation or request), ～から is used.

⑦ 危(あぶ)ないですから、機械(きかい)に 触(さわ)らないで ください。
Please don't touch the machine; it's dangerous.
×危(あぶ)なくて、機械(きかい)に 触(さわ)らないで ください。

2）N で

N で is often used with natural phenomena and events such as じこ (accidents), じしん (earthquakes) and かじ (fires):

⑧ 地震(じしん)で ビルが 倒(たお)れました。　The building fell down in an earthquake.

⑨ 病気(びょうき)で 会社(かいしゃ)を 休(やす)みました。　I got ill and took some time off work.

**2.**

| | | |
|---|---|---|
| **V**<br>い **-adj** | **plain form** | ので、～ |
| な **-adj**<br>**N** | **plain form**<br>～だ→～な | |

Like the ～から introduced in Lesson 9, ～ので also indicates a cause or reason. Since ので inherently possesses the characteristic of indicating a consequence (cause and result) and stating a result derived from a cause, it is suitable for softly expressing a reason or justification when asking permission for something:

⑩ 日本語が わからないので、英語で 話して いただけませんか。

I don't understand Japanese, so would you mind speaking in English?

⑪ 用事が あるので、お先に 失礼します。

There's something I need to do, so please excuse me for leaving before you.

**3.** 途中で

とちゅうで means 'during' or 'on the way to'. It is used in conjunction with the dictionary form of a verb or with N の .

⑫ 実は 来る 途中で 事故が あって、バスが 遅れて しまったんです。

In fact, there was an accident en route and the bus was late.

⑬ マラソンの 途中で 気分が 悪く なりました。

I felt ill during the marathon.

# Lesson 40

## I. Vocabulary

| | | |
|---|---|---|
| かぞえますⅡ | 数えます | count |
| はかりますⅠ | 測ります、量ります | measure, weigh |
| たしかめますⅡ | 確かめます | confirm, make sure |
| あいますⅠ<br>［サイズが～］ | 合います | [the size] fit |
| しゅっぱつしますⅢ* | 出発します | depart |
| とうちゃくしますⅢ | 到着します | arrive |
| よいますⅠ | 酔います | get drunk |
| うまく いきますⅠ | | go well |
| でますⅡ<br>［もんだいが～］ | 出ます<br>［問題が～］ | [problems] be on the test |
| そうだんしますⅢ | 相談します | consult, discuss |
| ひつよう［な］ | 必要［な］ | necessary |
| てんきよほう | 天気予報 | weather forecast |
| ぼうねんかい | 忘年会 | year-end party |
| しんねんかい* | 新年会 | New Year's party |
| にじかい | 二次会 | second party |
| はっぴょうかい | 発表会 | presentation meeting |
| たいかい | 大会 | rally, convention |
| マラソン | | marathon |
| コンテスト | | contest |
| おもて | 表 | face, front |
| うら* | 裏 | back (side) |
| まちがい | | mistake |
| きず | 傷 | defect, wound, scratch |
| ズボン | | trousers |
| ［お］としより | ［お］年寄り | elderly person |
| ながさ* | 長さ | length |
| おもさ | 重さ | weight |
| たかさ | 高さ | height |
| おおきさ* | 大きさ | size, scale |
| ［－］びん | ［－］便 | flight, flight number |
| －こ* | －個 | (counter for small objects) |
| －ほん<br>（－ぽん、－ぼん） | －本 | (counter for long objects) |
| －はい<br>（－ぱい、－ばい）* | －杯 | － glass or cup of (counter for full cups, glasses, etc.) |

| | | |
|---|---|---|
| －センチ* | | － centimetres |
| －ミリ* | | － millimetres |
| －グラム* | | － grammes |
| ～いじょう* | ～以上 | not less than ～, over ～ |
| ～いか | ～以下 | not more than ～, under ～ |
| | | |
| ※長崎（ながさき） | | capital of Nagasaki prefecture |
| ※仙台（せんだい） | | capital of Miyagi prefecture |
| ※JL | | Japan Airlines |
| ※七夕祭り（たなばたまつり） | | the Star Festival |
| ※東照宮（とうしょうぐう） | | shrine dedicated to Tokugawa Ieyasu in Nikko, Tochigi prefecture |

**〈会話（かいわ）〉**

| | |
|---|---|
| どうでしょうか。 | How is ～? (polite equivalent of どうですか) |
| テスト | test, examination |
| 成績（せいせき） | performance, score, result |
| ところで | by the way |
| いらっしゃいますＩ | come (respectful equivalent of きます) |
| 様子（ようす） | situation, condition, appearance |

**〈読み物（よみもの）〉**

| | |
|---|---|
| 事件（じけん） | incident, case |
| オートバイ | motorcycle |
| 爆弾（ばくだん） | bomb |
| 積（つ）みますＩ | load, pile up |
| 運転手（うんてんしゅ） | driver |
| 離（はな）れた | remote |
| 急（きゅう）に | suddenly |
| 動（うご）かしますＩ | start, operate, move |
| 一生懸命（いっしょうけんめい） | with all one's effort |
| 犯人（はんにん） | offender, criminal |
| 男（おとこ） | man |
| 手（て）に入（い）れますⅡ | obtain, get |
| 今（いま）でも | even now |

## II. Translation

### Sentence Patterns

1. Please find out what time flight JL 107 arrives.
2. They can't tell yet whether or not Typhoon No.9 will hit Tokyo.
3. May I try these clothes on?

### Example Sentences

1. Where did you go drinking next?
   ……I was drunk, so I have no idea where we went.
2. Do you know how to measure the height of a mountain?
   ……No, let's check on the Internet.
3. Do you remember when we first met?
   ……It was a long time ago, so I've forgotten.
4. Please reply by e-mail saying whether or not you can attend the year-end party.
   ……Yes, all right.
5. This is a document I have to submit to the University; would you mind checking it for me?
   ……No, I don't mind.
6. Have you ever been to Nagasaki?
   ……No, not yet. I would really like to go there one day.



### Conversation

**I'm worried about whether he's made any friends or not**

Klara: Ms. Ito, how is Hans getting on at school?
I'm worried about whether he's made any friends or not......
Ms. Ito: He's fine.
He's very popular with his classmates.
Klara: Really? I'm glad to hear it.
How is he getting on with his studies? He says he finds kanji difficult......
Ms. Ito: We have a kanji test every day, and Hans gets good marks.
Klara: Does he? Thank you very much.
Ms. Ito: By the way, it's Sports Day soon. Will Hans's father be coming too?
Klara: Yes.
Ms. Ito: Do please come and see what Hans is like at school.
Klara: We will. Thank you very much.

## III. Useful Words & Information

### 単位（たんい）・線（せん）・形（かたち）・模様（もよう）　Units, Lines, Shapes and Patterns

#### 面積（めんせき）　Area

| | | |
|---|---|---|
| $cm^2$ | 平方（へいほう）センチメートル | square centimetre |
| $m^2$ | 平方（へいほう）メートル | square metre |
| $km^2$ | 平方（へいほう）キロメートル | square kilometre |

#### 長さ（なが）　Length

| | | |
|---|---|---|
| mm | ミリ［メートル］ | millimetre |
| cm | センチ［メートル］ | centimetre |
| m | メートル | metre |
| km | キロ［メートル］ | kilometre |

#### 体積（たいせき）・容積（ようせき）　Volume and Capacity

| | | |
|---|---|---|
| $cm^3$ | 立方（りっぽう）センチメートル | cubic centimetre |
| $m^3$ | 立方（りっぽう）メートル | cubic metre |
| ml | ミリリットル | millilitre |
| cc | シーシー | cc |
| ℓ | リットル | litre |

#### 重さ（おも）　Weight

| | | |
|---|---|---|
| mg | ミリグラム | milligramme |
| g | グラム | gramme |
| kg | キロ［グラム］ | kilogramme |
| t | トン | tonne |

#### 計算（けいさん）　Calculation

$$1 + 2 - 3 \times 4 \div 6 = 1$$

| + | − | × | ÷ | = |
|---|---|---|---|---|
| たす | ひく | かける | わる | は（イコール） |
| plus | minus | multiplied by | divided by | equals |

95

#### 線（せん）　Lines

| | | |
|---|---|---|
| 直線（ちょくせん） | straight line | ―――――― |
| 曲線（きょくせん） | curved line | 〜〜〜 |
| 点線（てんせん） | dotted line | ………………… |

#### 形（かたち）　Shapes

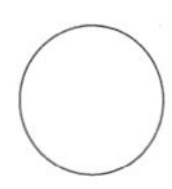
円（えん）（丸（まる））
circle

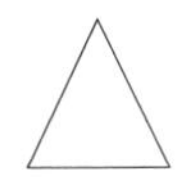
三角（さんかく）［形（けい）］
triangle

四角（しかく）［形（けい）］
square

40

#### 模様（もよう）　Patterns

縦（たて）じま
vertical stripes

横（よこ）じま
horizontal stripes

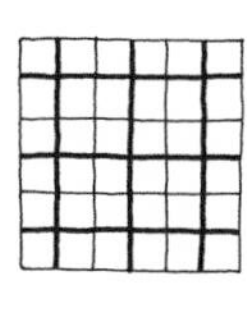
チェック
check

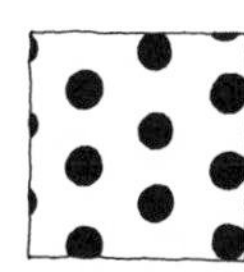
水玉（みずたま）
polka-dot

花柄（はながら）
floral print

無地（むじ）
plain

## IV. Grammar Notes

**1.**

| | | |
|---|---|---|
| **V**<br>**い -adj** | **plain form** | か、～ |
| **な -adj**<br>**N** | **plain form**<br>～だ | |

This sentence pattern is used when using a question that includes an interrogative as a component of another sentence:

① JL107便は 何時に 到着するか、調べて ください。

Please check what time flight JL107 arrives.

② 結婚の お祝いは 何が いいか、話して います。

We're talking about what to give as a wedding present.

③ わたしたちが 初めて 会ったのは いつか、覚えて いますか。

Do you remember when it was that we first met?

Since an interrogative is a noun, it takes the form 'interrogative か', as in Example ③.

**2.**

| | | |
|---|---|---|
| **V**<br>**い -adj** | **plain form** | か どうか、～ |
| **な -adj**<br>**N** | **plain form**<br>～だ | |



This sentence pattern is adopted when using a question that does not include an interrogative as a component of another sentence. Be careful, because どうか is required after plain form か.

④ 忘年会に 出席するか どうか、20日までに 返事を ください。

Please reply by the 20th, stating whether you will attend the year-end party or not.

⑤ その 話は ほんとうか どうか、わかりません。

I don't know whether that was true or not.

⑥ まちがいが ないか どうか、調べて ください。

Please check whether or not there are any mistakes.



The reason why it is まちがいが ないか どうか and not まちがいが あるか どうか in Example ⑥ is that the speaker wants to make sure there are no mistakes, not that there are some mistakes.

**3.** **V て-form みます**

This sentence pattern is used to indicate trying out an action:

⑦ もう 一度(いちど) 考(かんが)えて みます。

I'll have another think about it.

⑧ この ズボンを はいて みても いいですか。

May I try these trousers on?

⑨ 北海道(ほっかいどう)へ 行(い)って みたいです。

I'd like to go and see Hokkaido.

The form 〜て みたい can be used as in Example ⑨ to express more reticently something one hopes for than when using 〜たい.

**4.** **い-adj(〜~~い~~)→〜さ**

An い-adjective can be converted to a noun by changing the ending い to さ:

Examples: 高(たか)い → 高(たか)さ　長(なが)い → 長(なが)さ　速(はや)い → 速(はや)さ

⑩ 山(やま)の 高(たか)さは どうやって 測(はか)るか、知(し)って いますか。

Do you know how to measure the height of a mountain?

⑪ 新(あたら)しい 橋(はし)の 長(なが)さは 3,911 メートルです。

The new bridge is 3,911 metres long.

**5.** **〜でしょうか**

Using 〜でしょう (see Lesson 32) in an interrogative sentence as in Example ⑫ is a way of asking a question without demanding a definite answer, so it enables the speaker to give a softer impression to the listener:

⑫ ハンスは 学校(がっこう)で どうでしょうか。

How is Hans getting on at school?

# Lesson 41

## I. Vocabulary

| | | |
|---|---|---|
| いただきます I | | receive (humble equivalent of もらいます) |
| くださいます I | | give (respectful equivalent of くれます) |
| やります I | | give (to a younger person, subordinate, animals or plants) |
| あげます II | 上げます | raise, lift up |
| さげます II * | 下げます | lower, pull down |
| しんせつに します III | 親切に します | be kind to |
| かわいい | | lovely, cute |
| めずらしい | 珍しい | rare, uncommon |
| おいわい | お祝い | celebration, gift (～を します：celebrate) |
| おとしだま | お年玉 | money given as a New Year's gift |
| [お]みまい | [お]見舞い | expression of sympathy, consolatory gift to a sick person |
| きょうみ | 興味 | interest ([コンピューターに] ～が あります：be interested [in computers]) |
| じょうほう | 情報 | information |
| ぶんぽう | 文法 | grammar |
| はつおん | 発音 | pronunciation |
| さる | 猿 | ape, monkey |
| えさ | | feed, bait |
| おもちゃ | | toy |
| えほん | 絵本 | picture book |
| えはがき | 絵はがき | picture postcard |
| ドライバー | | screwdriver |
| ハンカチ | | handkerchief |
| くつした | 靴下 | socks, stockings |
| てぶくろ | 手袋 | gloves |
| ようちえん | 幼稚園 | preschool, kindergarten |
| だんぼう | 暖房 | heating |
| れいぼう * | 冷房 | air-conditioning |
| おんど | 温度 | temperature |

| | | |
|---|---|---|
| そふ* | 祖父 | (my) grandfather |
| そぼ | 祖母 | (my) grandmother |
| まご | 孫 | (my) grandchild |
| おまごさん | お孫さん | (someone else's) grandchild |
| おじ* | | (my) uncle |
| おじさん* | | (someone else's) uncle |
| おば | | (my) aunt |
| おばさん* | | (someone else's) aunt |
| かんりにん | 管理人 | janitor, caretaker |
| ～さん | | (suffix added to a person's job title as a polite way of referring to them) |
| このあいだ | この間 | the other day |

**〈会話(かいわ)〉**

| | |
|---|---|
| ひとこと | a few words |
| ～ずつ | each |
| 二人(ふたり) | couple |
| お宅(たく) | home (respectfull equivalent of うち or いえ) |
| どうぞ お幸(しあわ)せに。 | I hope you will be very happy. |

**〈読み物(よみもの)〉**

| | |
|---|---|
| 昔話(むかしばなし) | old tale, folklore |
| ある ～ | a certain ～, one ～ |
| 男(おとこ) | man |
| 子(こ)どもたち | children |
| いじめますⅡ | bully, abuse, ill-treat |
| かめ | turtle, tortoise |
| 助(たす)けますⅡ | save, help |
| 優(やさ)しい | kind, gentle, tender-hearted |
| お姫様(ひめさま) | princess |
| 暮(く)らしますⅠ | live, lead a life |
| 陸(りく) | land, shore |
| すると | and, then |
| 煙(けむり) | smoke |
| 真(ま)っ白(しろ)[な] | pure white |
| 中身(なかみ) | content |
| ※浦島太郎(うらしまたろう) | name of the main character in an old folk tale |

## II. Translation

### Sentence Patterns

1. I received a book from Professor Watt.
2. My teacher corrected my kanji mistakes for me.
3. My department manager's wife taught me the tea ceremony.
4. I made a paper aeroplane for my son.

### Example Sentences

1. This is a beautiful plate, isn't it?
   ……Yes. Mr. Tanaka gave it to us as a wedding gift.
2. Mummy, can I give the monkey a sweet?
   ……No. That sign over there says you mustn't give them any food, doesn't it?
3. Have you ever been to see sumo?
   ……Yes. The department manager took me there recently.
   It was very interesting.
4. How was your summer holiday homestay?
   ……I enjoyed it. The whole family treated me very kindly.
5. What are you going to do during the holidays?
   ……I'm going to take my children to Disneyland.
6. I don't really understand how to use the new copier.
   Would you mind showing me?
   ……Sure.



### Conversation

**Congratulations on your wedding**

Chancellor: Professor Watt and Izumi, congratulations on your wedding. Cheers!

Everyone: Cheers!

……………………………………………………

MC: Now I would like to ask everyone here to say a few words.

Yoshiko Matsumoto: I was taught English by Professor Watt in class last summer. His lessons were humorous and enjoyable. As a matter of fact, Izumi was also in that class.

University staff member: I received a book called 'How to Organise Effectively' from Professor Watt. He is very good at organising things, and his office is always tidy. I think the couple's home will definitely be excellent too.

Miller: Professor Watt, next would you be so kind as to write a book entitled 'How to Get Married to a Wonderful Person?'
I would really like to read and learn from it. I hope you will be very happy.

## III. Useful Words & Information

### 便利情報　Useful Information

貸衣装の「みんなの晴れ着」
'Festive Dress for Everyone' Clothes for Hire

何でもそろいます!!　新作がいっぱい!!
We Have Clothes for All Occasions!　Many brand-new outfits!

☎ 03-3812-556×

| | |
|---|---|
| 七五三 | Celebration for 7, 5 and 3 year-old children |
| 卒業式 | Graduation Ceremonies |
| 成人式 | Coming-of-Age Ceremonies |
| 結婚式 | Weddings |

泊まりませんか
Why not come and stay with us?

民宿 三浦
Miura Guest House

安い、親切、家庭的な宿
Nice accommodation with a friendly atmosphere and attentive service at affordable prices.

☎ 0585-214-1234

公民館からのお知らせ　Communitiy Centre Information

| | | | |
|---|---|---|---|
| 月曜日 | Mon. | 日本料理講習会 | Japanese cooking class |
| 火曜日 | Tue. | 生け花スクール | Flower arrangement class |
| 水曜日 | Wed. | 日本語教室 | Japanese language class |

＊毎月第３日曜日　On the 3rd Sun. of every month　バザー　Bazaar

☎ 0798-72-251×

便利屋　Helping Hands
☎ 0343-885-8854

何でもします!!
Leave everything to us!

☆家の修理、掃除
House repairs, house cleaning
☆赤ちゃん、子どもの世話
Baby-sitting
☆犬の散歩
Dog walking
☆話し相手
Companion service

レンタルサービス
Rental Service

何でも貸します!!
Rent anything and everything

| | |
|---|---|
| ・カラオケ | Karaoke sets |
| ・ビデオカメラ | Video cameras |
| ・携帯電話 | Mobile phones |
| ・ベビー用品 | Baby goods |
| ・レジャー用品 | Recreational equipment |
| ・旅行用品 | Travel goods |

☎ 0741-41-5151

お寺で体験できます
Try the following at our temple:

| | |
|---|---|
| 禅ができます | Zen meditation |
| 精進料理が食べられます | Traditional Buddhist vegetarian cuisine |

金銀寺　☎ 0562-231-2010

## IV. Grammar Notes

### 1. Expressions for giving and receiving

Lessons 7 and 24 introduced expressions for the giving and receiving of things and actions. This lesson introduces different expressions for the giving and receiving of things and actions which reflect the relationship between the giver and the receiver.

1) $N_1$(person)に $N_2$を いただきます

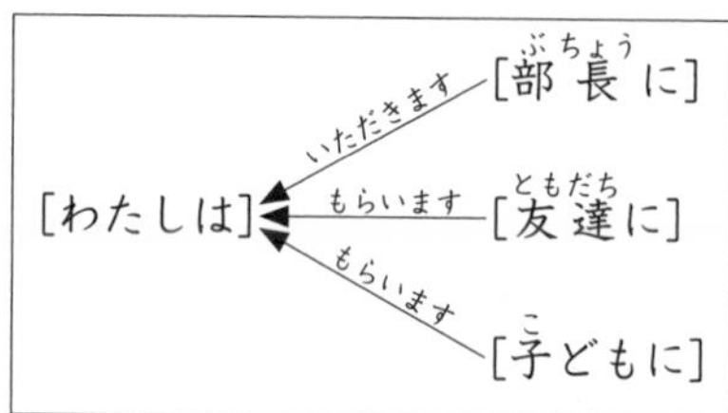


When the speaker receives something ($N_2$) from someone of higher status ($N_1$), いただきます is used rather than もらいます:

① わたしは 社長に お土産を いただきました。

I received a souvenir from the company president.

2) [わたしに] Nを くださいます

[部長が] くださいます
[友達が] くれます
[子どもが] くれます
[わたしに]

When someone of higher status gives the speaker something, くださいます is used rather than くれます:

② 社長が わたしに お土産を くださいました。

The company president gave me a souvenir.

[Note] いただきます and くださいます are also used when the recipient is related to the speaker:

③ 娘は 部長に お土産を いただきました。

My daughter received a souvenir from the Department Manager.

④ 部長が 娘に お土産を くださいました。

The Department Manager gave my daughter a souvenir.

3) $N_1$に $N_2$を やります

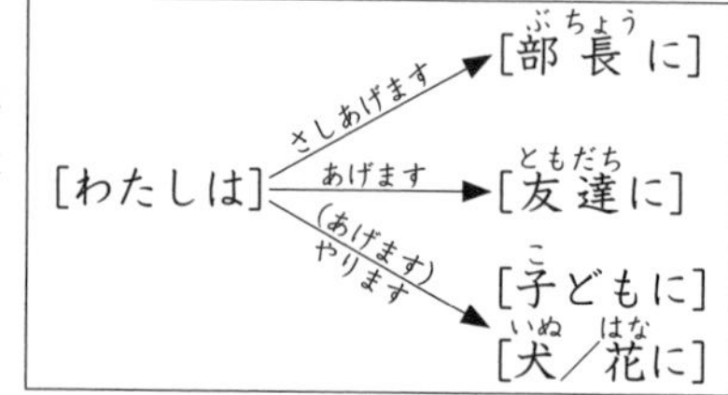


When the recipient is someone of lower status, an animal or a plant, やります should really be used, but these days many people prefer to use あげます as it sounds more polite:

⑤ わたしは 息子に お菓子を やりました（あげました）。

I gave my son some sweets.

⑥ わたしは 犬に えさを やりました。

I gave the dog some food.

## 2. Giving and receiving of actions

いただきます, くださいます and やります are also used for expressing the giving and receiving of actions, as in the following examples:

1) V て -form いただきます

⑦ わたしは 課長に 手紙の まちがいを 直して いただきました。

The Section Manager corrected the mistakes in my letter for me.

2) V て -form くださいます

⑧ 部長の 奥さんが [わたしに] お茶を 教えて くださいました。

The Department Manager's wife taught me how to perform the tea ceremony.

⑨ 部長が [わたしを] 駅まで 送って くださいました。

The Department Manager took me to the station.

⑩ 部長が [わたしの] レポートを 直して くださいました。

The Department Manager corrected my report for me.

3) V て -form やります

⑪ わたしは 息子に 紙飛行機を 作って やりました (あげました)。

I made a paper aeroplane for my son.

⑫ わたしは 犬を 散歩に 連れて 行って やりました。

I took my dog for a walk.

⑬ わたしは 娘の 宿題を 見て やりました (あげました)。

I checked my daughter's homework for her.

## 3. V て -form くださいませんか

This way of making a request is politer than ～て ください but not as polite as ～て いただけませんか, which was introduced in Lesson 26.

⑭ コピー機の 使い方を 教えて くださいませんか。

Would you mind teaching me how to use the copier?

⑮ コピー機の 使い方を 教えて いただけませんか。

Would you be so kind as to teach me how to use the copier? (See Lesson 26)

## 4. N に V

When used as illustrated in the following two examples, the particle に means 'as a token of' or 'in memory of':

⑯ 田中さんが 結婚祝いに この お皿を くださいました。

Mr. Tanaka gave us this dish as a wedding gift.

⑰ 北海道旅行の お土産に 人形を 買いました。

I bought a doll as a souvenir of my trip to Hokkaido.

# Lesson 42

## I. Vocabulary

| | | |
|---|---|---|
| つつみますⅠ | 包みます | wrap |
| わかしますⅠ | 沸かします | boil |
| まぜますⅡ | 混ぜます | mix |
| けいさんしますⅢ | 計算します | calculate |
| ならびますⅠ | 並びます | stand in a queue, line up |
| じょうぶ[な] | 丈夫[な] | strong, healthy |
| アパート | | apartment, flat |
| べんごし | 弁護士 | lawyer, attorney, solicitor, barrister |
| おんがくか | 音楽家 | musician |
| こどもたち | 子どもたち | children |
| しぜん | 自然 | nature |
| きょういく | 教育 | education |
| ぶんか | 文化 | culture |
| しゃかい | 社会 | society |
| せいじ | 政治 | politics |
| ほうりつ | 法律 | law |
| せんそう* | 戦争 | war |
| へいわ | 平和 | peace |
| もくてき | 目的 | purpose |
| ろんぶん | 論文 | thesis, academic paper |
| たのしみ | 楽しみ | pleasure, enjoyment, expectation |
| ミキサー | | mixer, blender |
| やかん | | kettle |
| ふた | | lid, cover, cap |
| せんぬき | 栓抜き | bottle opener, corkscrew |
| かんきり | 缶切り | can opener |
| かんづめ | 缶詰 | canned food, tinned food |
| のしぶくろ | のし袋 | envelope for a gift of money |
| ふろしき | | wrapping cloth used to carry things |
| そろばん | | abacus |
| たいおんけい | 体温計 | (clinical) thermometer |
| ざいりょう | 材料 | material, ingredient |
| ある ～ | | a certain ～, one ～ |
| いっしょうけんめい | 一生懸命 | with all one's effort |
| なぜ | | why |

| | |
|---|---|
| どのくらい | how much, how many |
| ※国連（こくれん） | United Nations |
| ※エリーゼの ために | Für Elise (For Elise) |
| ※ベートーベン | Ludwig van Beethoven, German composer (1770-1827) |
| ※こどもニュース | a fictitious news programme |

**〈会話（かいわ）〉**

| | |
|---|---|
| 出（で）ますII［ボーナスが～］ | [bonus] be paid |
| 半分（はんぶん） | half |
| ローン | loan |

**〈読み物（よみもの）〉**

| | |
|---|---|
| カップめん | instant noodles sold in a ready-to-use disposable container, pot noodles |
| 世界初（せかいはつ） | world's first |
| ～に よって | by ～ |
| どんぶり | bowl |
| めん | noodles |
| 広（ひろ）めますII | spread |
| 市場調査（しじょうちょうさ） | market survey, market research |
| 割（わ）りますI | break |
| 注（そそ）ぎますI | pour |
| ※チキンラーメン | brand name of instant noodles |
| ※安藤百福（あんどうももふく） | Japanese businessman and inventor (1910-2007) |

## II. Translation

### Sentence Patterns

1. I'm saving so that I can have my own shop in the future.
2. These boots are good for walking in the mountains.

### Example Sentences

1. I'm practising every day so that I can take part in the Bon dances.
   ……Are you? That's exciting, isn't it?
2. Why do you go climbing in the mountains on your own?
   ……I go to the mountains to be alone and meditate.
3. Are you doing anything for your health?
   ……No, but I'm thinking of going jogging every morning, starting next week.
4. That's a beautiful piece, isn't it?
   ……It's 'Für Elise'. Beethoven wrote it for a woman.
5. What's this used for?
   ……It's used for opening wine.
6. Do you have a bag suitable for a two-to-three-day business trip?
   ……How about this one? You can get a laptop in it too, so it's handy.
7. How many years did it take to build this bridge?
   ……[It took] twelve [years].



### Conversation

**What are you going to spend your bonus on?**

Suzuki: Ms. Hayashi, when do you get your bonus?
Hayashi: Next week. How about your company?
Suzuki: Tomorrow. Exciting, isn't it?
Hayashi: Yes. How are you going to use yours?
Suzuki: First I'm going to buy a new bicycle, then I'm going to go on a trip.......
Ogawa: Aren't you going to save any?
Suzuki: I hadn't really thought about that.
Hayashi: I'm planning to save half.
Suzuki: What? You're going to save as much as half?
Hayashi: Yes, I'd like to visit the UK to study one day.
Ogawa: It's all right for you single people, isn't it? You can spend it all on yourselves. Once I've paid the mortgage and saved some for my children's education fees, there'll be hardly any left, you know.

## III. Useful Words & Information

### 事務用品(じむようひん)・道具(どうぐ)　Office Supplies and Tools

| | | | |
|---|---|---|---|
| とじる<br>staple | 挟(はさ)む／とじる<br>clip | 留(と)める<br>pin, tack | 切(き)る<br>cut |
|  ホッチキス<br>stapler | 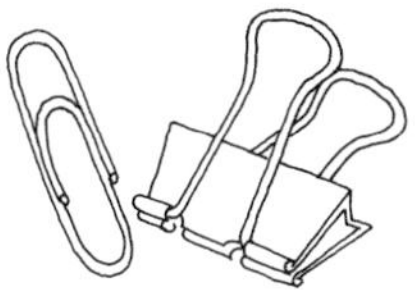 クリップ<br>clip | 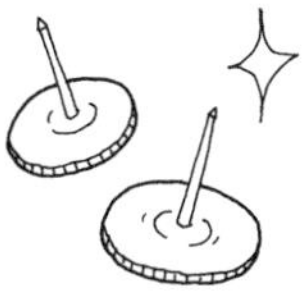 画(が)びょう<br>drawing pin | 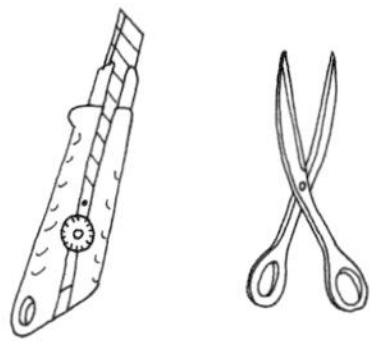 カッター　はさみ<br>cutter　scissors |
| はる<br>stick, paste | | 削(けず)る<br>sharpen | ファイルする<br>file |
| 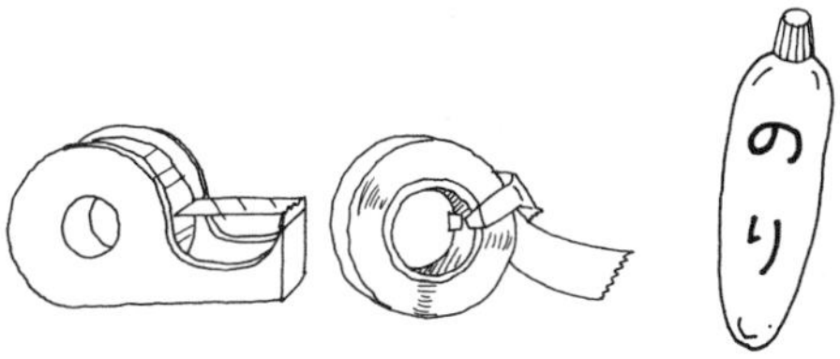 セロテープ　ガムテープ<br>Sellotape　packaging tape | のり<br>glue |  鉛筆削(えんぴつけず)り<br>pencil sharpener |  ファイル<br>file |
| 消(け)す<br>erase | [穴(あな)を] 開(あ)ける<br>punch | 計算(けいさん)する<br>calculate | [線(せん)を] 引(ひ)く／測(はか)る<br>draw [a line]/measure |
|  消(け)しゴム　修正液(しゅうせいえき)<br>eraser　correction fluid | 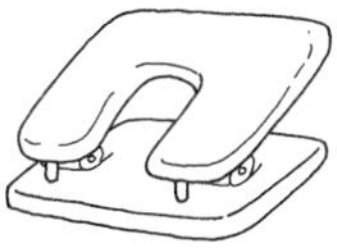 パンチ<br>punch | 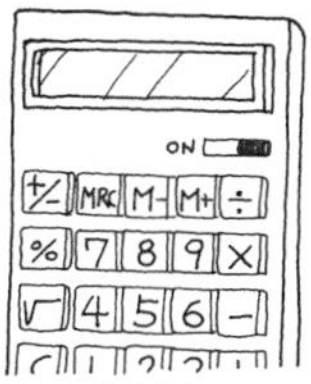 電卓(でんたく)<br>calculator |  定規(じょうぎ)(物差(ものさ)し)<br>ruler |
| 切(き)る<br>saw | [くぎを] 打(う)つ<br>hit [a nail] | 挟(はさ)む／曲(ま)げる／切(き)る<br>pinch/bend/cut | [ねじを]締(し)める／緩(ゆる)める<br>tighten/loosen<br>[a screw] |
|  のこぎり<br>saw |  金(かな)づち<br>hammer | 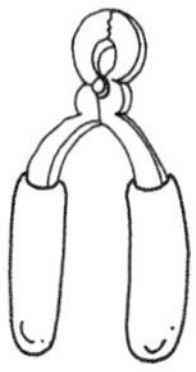 ペンチ<br>pliers |  ドライバー<br>screwdriver |

## IV. Grammar Notes

**1.** | V dictionary form<br>Nの | ために、～ | in order to V<br>for N |
|---|---|---|

ために indicates a purpose. Nの ために may also be used in the sense of ‘for the benefit of N’, as in Example ④ .

① 自分の 店を 持つ ために、貯金して います。

I'm saving up in order to get my own shop.

② 引っ越しの ために、車を 借ります。

I'm going to rent a van for the move.

③ 健康の ために、毎朝 走って います。

I run every day for my health.

④ 家族の ために、うちを 建てます。

I'm going to build a house for my family.

[Note 1] The similar expression ～ように was introduced in Lesson 36, but, while the dictionary form of a volitional verb is used in front of ために , the dictionary form of a non-volitional verb or the negative form of a verb is used in front of ように .

Comparing the two sentences below, while ① says that the speaker is saving up in order to get his or her own shop, ⑤ says that the speaker is saving up in order to create a situation in which he or she will become able to have his or her own shop:



① 自分の 店を 持つ ために、貯金して います。

I'm saving up in order to get my own shop.

⑤ 自分の 店が 持てるように、貯金して います。

I'm saving up so I can have my own shop.

[Note 2] なります can be used as both a volitional verb and a non-volitional verb:

⑥ 弁護士に なる ために、法律を 勉強して います。

I'm studying law in order to become a solicitor.

⑦ 日本語が 上手に なるように、毎日 勉強して います。

I'm studying every day so I will become good at Japanese. (See Lesson 36)

**2.** | V dictionary formの<br>N | に ～ |
|---|---|

This sentence pattern is used together with phrases such as つかいます , いいです , べんりです , やくに たちます and [じかん]が かかります in order to indicate their application or purpose:



⑧ この はさみは 花を 切るのに 使います。

These scissors are used for cutting flowers.

⑨ この かばんは 大きくて、旅行に 便利です。

This suitcase is large, and useful for travelling.

⑩ 電話番号を 調べるのに 時間が かかりました。

It took a long time to find the telephone number.

## 3. Quantifier は／も

When the particle は is attached to a quantifier, it indicates that the speaker thinks that the amount mentioned is a minimum. When the particle も is attached to a quantifier, it indicates that the speaker thinks that the amount mentioned is large:

⑪ わたしは ［ボーナスの］ 半分(はんぶん)は 貯金(ちょきん)する つもりです。
……えっ、半分(はんぶん)も 貯金(ちょきん)するんですか。
I intend to save [at least] half [of my bonus].
…… Really? You're going to save as much as half?

## 4. ～に よって

When a verb expressing creation or discovery ( かきます , はつめいします , はっけんします , etc.) is used in the passive, the agent is indicated by に よって , not by に :

⑫ チキンラーメンは 1958年(ねん)に 安藤百福(あんどうももふく)さんに よって 発明(はつめい)されました。
Chicken ramen was invented by Momofuku Ando in 1958.

# Lesson 43

## I. Vocabulary

| | | |
|---|---|---|
| ふえますⅡ<br>［ゆしゅつが～］ | 増えます<br>［輸出が～］ | [exports] increase |
| へりますⅠ<br>［ゆしゅつが～］ | 減ります<br>［輸出が～］ | [exports] decrease |
| あがりますⅠ<br>［ねだんが～］ | 上がります<br>［値段が～］ | [the price] rise |
| さがりますⅠ*<br>［ねだんが～］ | 下がります<br>［値段が～］ | [the price] fall, drop |
| きれますⅡ<br>［ひもが～］ | 切れます | [a string] break, snap |
| とれますⅡ<br>［ボタンが～］ | | [a button] come off |
| おちますⅡ<br>［にもつが～］ | 落ちます<br>［荷物が～］ | [baggage] fall down |
| なくなりますⅠ<br>［ガソリンが～］ | | [petrol, gasoline] run out, be lost |
| へん［な］ | 変［な］ | strange, peculiar |
| しあわせ［な］ | 幸せ［な］ | happy |
| らく［な］ | 楽［な］ | easy |
| うまい* | | tasty |
| まずい | | not tasty |
| つまらない | | boring, uninteresting, trivial |
| やさしい | 優しい | kind, gentle, tender-hearted |
| ガソリン | | petrol, gasoline |
| ひ | 火 | fire |
| パンフレット | | pamphlet |
| いまにも | 今にも | at any moment (used to describe a situation just before it changes) |
| わあ | | Oh!/Wow! |

**〈読み物(よみもの)〉**

| | |
|---|---|
| ばら | rose |
| ドライブ | driving |
| 理由(りゆう) | reason |
| 謝(あやま)りますＩ | apologize |
| 知(し)り合(あ)いますＩ | get acquainted |

## II. Translation

### Sentence Patterns

1. It looks like it's going to rain soon.
2. I'll just go and buy a ticket.

### Example Sentences

1. Your jacket button looks as if it's about to come off.
   ……Oh, so it does. Thank you very much.
2. It's got warmer, hasn't it?
   ……Yes, it feels as if the cherry blossoms will be out soon, doesn't it?
3. This is a German apple cake. Please try a piece.
   ……Wow, it looks delicious! Thank you.
4. This part-time job looks great, doesn't it? The pay's good and the work looks easy.
   ……But it's from twelve at night until six in the morning, you know.
5. There aren't enough copies, are there?
   ……How many more do we need? I'll go and get some right away.
6. I'm just going out for a while.
   ……About what time will you be back?
   I'm planning to be back by 4 o'clock.



### Conversation

**He seems to be enjoying himself every day**

Hayashi: Who's this a photograph of?
Schmidt: It's my son, Hans. I took it at his Sports Day.
Hayashi: He looks well, doesn't he?
Schmidt: Yes. Hans can run fast.
He's got used to being at Japanese elementary school, he's made friends, and he seems to be enjoying himself every day.
Hayashi: That's good, isn't it?
Is this your wife? She's beautiful, isn't she?
Schmidt: Thank you. She's interested in lots of different things, and she's fun to be with.
Hayashi: Is she?
Schmidt: She particularly likes history, and she explores old towns when she has time to.

## III. Useful Words & Information

### 性格(せいかく)・性質(せいしつ)　Personality and Nature

| | |
|---|---|
| 明(あか)るい | cheerful |
| 暗(くら)い | gloomy |
| 優(やさ)しい | kind, gentle, tender-hearted |
| おとなしい | quiet, gentle |
| 冷(つめ)たい | cold |
| 厳(きび)しい | strict, severe |
| 気(き)が長(なが)い | slow-tempered, patient |
| 気(き)が短(みじか)い | quick-tempered |
| 気(き)が強(つよ)い | strong-willed |
| 気(き)が弱(よわ)い | timid |

| | |
|---|---|
| 活発(かっぱつ)[な] | active |
| 誠実(せいじつ)[な] | sincere |
| わがまま[な] | selfish |
| まじめ[な] | serious, earnest |
| ふまじめ[な] | frivolous |
| 頑固(がんこ)[な] | stubborn |
| 素直(すなお)[な] | obedient, gentle |
| 意地悪(いじわる)[な] | ill-natured, spiteful |
| 勝(か)ち気(き)[な] | competitive, unyielding |
| 神経質(しんけいしつ)[な] | highly-strung, nervous |

## IV. Grammar Notes

### 1. ～そうです looks like ～

1) V ます -form そうです

This sentence pattern expresses the speaker's belief that the movement or change indicated by the verb is likely to occur. It can be used with an adverb such as いまにも, もうすぐ or これから indicating a time frame:

① 今(いま)にも 雨(あめ)が 降(ふ)りそうです。　It looks like it's going to rain any moment.

② もうすぐ 桜(さくら)が 咲(さ)きそうです。
It looks like the cherry blossoms will come out soon.

③ これから 寒(さむ)く なりそうです。　It feels as if it's going to get colder.

2) い -adj(～い̸) / な -adj[な̸] } そうです

This expression is used when inferring the nature of something from its external appearance, without having actually confirmed that inference:

④ この 料理(りょうり)は 辛(から)そうです。　This dish looks spicy.

⑤ 彼女(かのじょ)は 頭(あたま)が よさそうです。　She seems intelligent.

⑥ この 机(つくえ)は 丈夫(じょうぶ)そうです。　This desk looks solid.

[Note] An adjective expressing feelings ( うれしい, かなしい, さびしい, etc.) cannot be used without modification when describing someone else's feelings; そうです must be attached to the adjective in order to indicate that the speaker is necessarily inferring what the person is feeling from their external appearance:

⑦ うれしそうですね。
……ええ、実(じつ)は きのう 結婚(けっこん)を 申(もう)し込(こ)まれたんです。
You seem happy, don't you?
…… Yes, as a matter of fact, I was proposed to yesterday.

### 2. V て -form 来(き)ます

1) V て -form きます indicates that the speaker is going to go somewhere, do something, and come back:

⑧ ちょっと たばこを 買(か)って 来(き)ます。
I'm just popping out to buy some cigarettes.

Example ⑧ indicates that the speaker is going to perform three actions: (1) go somewhere cigarettes are sold, (2) buy some cigarettes there, and (3) return to his or her starting point.

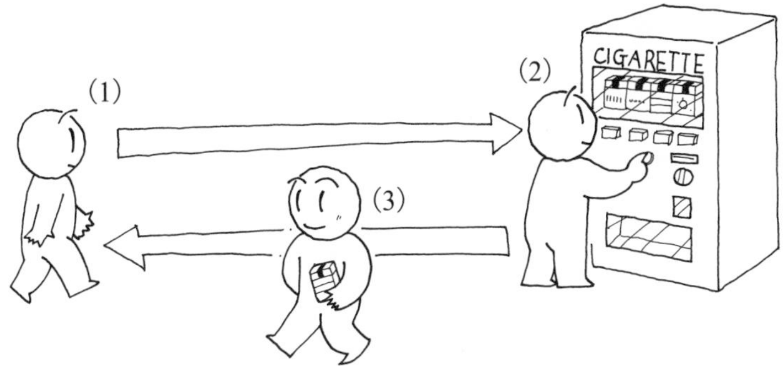


The place where the action indicated by V て -form is performed is marked by で , as in Example ⑨ , but から is used when that place is taken as the point of origin of what is indicated by を , as in Example ⑩ . Verbs such as もって きます and はこんで きます can also be used as well as とって きます as the verb used with から :

⑨ スーパーで 牛乳を 買って 来ます。

I'll go and buy some milk from the supermarket.

⑩ 台所から コップを 取って 来ます。

I'll get a glass from the kitchen.

2) N(place)へ 行って 来ます

The て -form of the verb いきます is used before きます to indicate that the speaker is going somewhere and then coming back. It is used when the speaker is saying nothing in particular about what he or she will do at the place he or she is going to:

⑪ 郵便局へ 行って 来ます。

I'm going to the post office [and coming back].

3) 出かけて 来ます

The て -form of the verb でかけます is used before きます to indicate that the speaker is going out somewhere and then coming back. It is used when the speaker is saying nothing in particular either about where he or she is going or what he or she intends to do there.

⑫ ちょっと 出かけて 来ます。　　I'm just popping out for a moment.

## 3. **V て -form くれませんか** Could you ～?

This is a politer expression than ～て ください , but not as polite as ～て いただけませんか (see Lesson 26) or ～て くださいませんか (see Lesson 41). It is appropriate when speaking to someone of equal or lower status than oneself:

⑬ コンビニへ 行って 来ます。
……じゃ、お弁当を 買って 来て くれませんか。

I'm going to the convenience store.
…… In that case, could you buy me a boxed meal?

# Lesson 44

## I. Vocabulary

| | | |
|---|---|---|
| なきます I | 泣きます | cry |
| わらいます I | 笑います | laugh, smile |
| ねむります I | 眠ります | sleep |
| かわきます I<br>［シャツが～］ | 乾きます | [a shirt] dry |
| ぬれます II*<br>［シャツが～］ | | [a shirt] get wet |
| すべります I | 滑ります | slip |
| おきます II<br>［じこが～］ | 起きます<br>［事故が～］ | [an accident] happen |
| ちょうせつします III | 調節します | adjust |
| あんぜん［な］ | 安全［な］ | safe |
| きけん［な］* | 危険［な］ | dangerous |
| こい | 濃い | strong (taste), dark (colour), thick (liquid) |
| うすい | 薄い | weak (taste), light (colour), thin |
| あつい | 厚い | thick |
| ふとい | 太い | thick (of large diameter) |
| ほそい* | 細い | thin (of small diameter) |
| くうき | 空気 | air |
| なみだ | 涙 | tear |
| わしょく | 和食 | Japanese dish |
| ようしょく | 洋食 | Western dish |
| おかず* | | side dish |
| りょう | 量 | quantity |
| －ばい | －倍 | － times |
| シングル | | single room |
| ツイン | | twin-bedded room |
| せんたくもの | 洗濯物 | washing, laundry |
| DVD | | DVD |
| ※ホテルひろしま | | a fictitious hotel |

**〈会話(かいわ)〉**

| | |
|---|---|
| どう　なさいますか。 | What can I do for you? (respectful) |
| カット | haircut |
| シャンプー | shampoo (～を　します：shampoo) |
| どういうふうに　なさいますか。 | How would you like it done? (respectful) |
| ショート | short |
| ～みたいに　して　ください。 | Do it like ～. |
| これで　よろしいでしょうか。 | Would this be all right? (polite) |
| [どうも] お疲(つか)れさまでした。 | Thank you for your patience. (shop assistant to customer) |

**〈読(よ)み物(もの)〉**

| | |
|---|---|
| 嫌(いや)がります I | dislike |
| また | and |
| うまく | well |
| 順序(じゅんじょ) | order |
| 安心(あんしん)[な] | relieved |
| 表現(ひょうげん) | expression |
| 例(たと)えば | for example |
| 別(わか)れます II | part, separate |
| これら | these |
| 縁起(えんぎ)が　悪(わる)い | unlucky, ill-omened |

## II. Translation

### Sentence Patterns

1. I drank too much last night.
2. This PC is easy to use.
3. Please shorten these trousers.

### Example Sentences

1. Are you crying?
   ……No, I laughed so much my eyes watered.
2. Modern cars are easy to drive, aren't they?
   ……Yes, but they're so easy that driving is no fun.
3. Which is nicer to live in; the countryside, or the town?
   ……I think the countryside's nicer, because prices are lower and the air is cleaner.
4. This glass is tough and doesn't break easily.
   ……It's safe for children to use, so it's good, isn't it?
5. It's already late in the evening; would you mind being quiet, please?
   ……Yes, I'm sorry.
6. What would you like to drink?
   ……I'll have a beer.



### Conversation

**Please do it like in this photograph**

Beautician: Good morning. (lit. Welcome.) What can we do for you today?
Lee: A haircut, please.
Beautician: Right then, I'll give you a shampoo first. This way, please.
……………………………………………………
Beautician: How would you like me to cut it?
Lee: I'd like it short, but......
Please do it like in this photograph.
Beautician: Oh, that's lovely, isn't it?
……………………………………………………
Beautician: Is the length in the front okay like this?
Lee: Hmm. Please make it a bit shorter.
……………………………………………………
Beautician: Thank you very much.
Lee: Thank you.

## III. Useful Words & Information

### 美容院（びよういん）・理髪店（りはつてん）　Beauty Salon and Barber's Shop

| | |
|---|---|
| カット | haircut |
| パーマ | perm |
| シャンプー | shampoo |
| トリートメント | treatment |
| ブロー | blow-dry |
| カラー | hair colouring |
| エクステ | hair extension |

| | |
|---|---|
| ネイル | nail care |
| フェイシャルマッサージ | facial massage |
| メイク | makeup |
| 着付（きつ）け | (kimono) dressing |

| | | |
|---|---|---|
| 耳（みみ）が見（み）えるくらいに | 切（き）ってください。 Please cut it | to just above the ears. |
| 肩（かた）にかかるくらいに | | to shoulder length. |
| まゆが隠（かく）れるくらいに | | so that my eyebrows are covered. |
| １センチくらい | | about one centimetre. |
| この写真（しゃしん）みたいに | | like in this photograph. |

| | | | |
|---|---|---|---|
| 髪（かみ）をとかす | comb one's hair | ひげ／顔（かお）をそる | shave |
| 髪（かみ）を分（わ）ける | part one's hair | 化粧（けしょう）／メイクする | put on makeup |
| 髪（かみ）をまとめる | gather one's hair | 三（み）つ編（あ）みにする | braid, plait |
| 髪（かみ）をアップにする | put one's hair up | 刈（か）り上（あ）げる | trim |
| 髪（かみ）を染（そ）める | dye one's hair | パーマをかける | perm |

## IV. Grammar Notes

**1.**

| | |
|---|---|
| **V ます -form**<br>**い -adj (～𝑖)**<br>**な -adj [な]** | すぎます |

～すぎます indicates that the extent of an action or state is excessive, and is therefore usually used when that action or state is undesirable:

① ゆうべ お酒を 飲みすぎました。 I drank too much last night.

② この セーターは 大きすぎます。 This sweater is too big for me.

[Note] ～すぎます conjugates like a Group II verb:

Examples: のみすぎる　　のみすぎ(ない)　　のみすぎた

③ 最近の 車は 操作が 簡単すぎて、運転が おもしろくないです。
Modern cars are no fun; they're too easy to drive.

④ いくら 好きでも、飲みすぎると、体に 悪いですよ。
No matter how much you like it, drinking too much is bad for your health.

**2.**

| | |
|---|---|
| **V ます -form** | やすいです<br>にくいです |

1) When V ます -form is a volitional verb, ～やすい means that it is easy to carry out the action indicated, while ～にくい means that it is difficult to carry it out:

⑤ この パソコンは 使いやすいです。
This PC is easy to use.

⑥ 東京は 住みにくいです。　　Tokyo is a hard place to live.

While Example ⑤ conveys the speaker's opinion that the PC has the attribute of being able to be used easily, Example ⑥ states that he or she thinks that living in the city of Tokyo is difficult.

2) When V ます -form is a non-volitional verb, ～やすい means that the action indicated by the verb is likely to occur, while ～にくい means that the action indicated by the verb is unlikely to occur:

⑦ 白い シャツは 汚れやすいです。 White shirts get dirty easily.

⑧ 雨の 日は 洗濯物が 乾きにくいです。
Washing doesn't dry easily on rainy days.

[Note] ～やすい and ～にくい decline like い -adjectives:

⑨ この 薬は 砂糖を 入れると、飲みやすく なりますよ。
This medicine is easier to take if you add some sugar.

⑩ この コップは 割れにくくて、安全ですよ。
This glass won't break easily, so it's safe.

**3.**

$N_1$を { い-adj（〜~~い~~）→〜く ／ な-adj［~~な~~］→〜に ／ $N_2$に } します

While 〜く／〜に なります (introduced in Lesson 19) expresses a change in the subject of a sentence, 〜く／〜に します indicates changing its object ($N_1$).

⑪ 音(おと)を 大(おお)きく します。　I'll turn the volume up.

⑫ 部屋(へや)を きれいに します。　I'll clean my room.

⑬ 塩(しお)の 量(りょう)を 半分(はんぶん)に しました。　I halved the amount of salt.

**4.**

**N**に します

This sentence pattern indicates a choice or decision:

⑭ 部屋(へや)は シングルに しますか、ツインに しますか。
Would you like a single room, or a twin?

⑮ 会議(かいぎ)は あしたに します。　We'll have the meeting tomorrow.

# Lesson 45

## I. Vocabulary

| | | |
|---|---|---|
| しんじますⅡ | 信じます | believe, trust |
| キャンセルしますⅢ | | cancel |
| しらせますⅡ | 知らせます | inform |
| ほしょうしょ | 保証書 | guarantee |
| りょうしゅうしょ | 領収書 | receipt |
| キャンプ | | camp |
| ちゅうし | 中止 | calling off, cancelling, suspension |
| てん | 点 | point, score |
| うめ | 梅 | plum (blossom) |
| 110ばん | 110番 | the emergency police telephone number |
| 119ばん | 119番 | the emergency fire service telephone number |
| きゅうに | 急に | suddenly |
| むりに | 無理に | unreasonably |
| たのしみに して います | 楽しみに して います | be looking forward to, be expecting |
| いじょうです。 | 以上です。 | That's all. |

**〈会話〉**

| | |
|---|---|
| 係員 | person in charge, organiser |
| コース | course, route |
| スタート | start |
| ー位 | -th (ranking) |
| 優勝しますⅢ | win the championship, come first |

**〈読み物〉**

| | |
|---|---|
| 悩み | trouble, worry |
| 目覚まし[時計] | alarm clock |
| 目が 覚めますⅡ | wake up |
| 大学生 | university student |
| 回答 | answer, reply (～します：answer, reply) |
| 鳴りますⅠ | ring |
| セットしますⅢ | set |
| それでも | nevertheless, for all that |

## II. Translation

### Sentence Patterns

1. If you lose your card, please contact your card company right away.
2. Although we had arranged to meet, she didn't come.

### Example Sentences

1. If the trains have stopped running because of an earthquake, please don't go out of your way to come home; stay at the office.
   ……OK, I will.
2. This is the guarantee for this computer.
   If anything goes wrong with it, please ring this number.
   ……Yes, I understand.
3. Excuse me, can one get receipts for photocopying charges at this library?
   ……Yes, please tell us if you need one.
4. Please do not use the lifts on any account in the event of a fire or an earthquake.
   ……Yes, I understand.
5. Did your speech go well?
   ……No, although I practised hard and learnt it by heart, I forgot it in the middle.
6. The cherry blossoms are out even though it's winter, aren't they?
   ……What? Those aren't cherry blossoms, you know. They're plum blossoms.



### Conversation

**What should we do if we go the wrong way?**

Organiser: This is a Health Marathon, everybody, so please don't overdo it.
If you don't feel well, please tell one of the organisers.
Participants: All right.
Participant 1: Excuse me, what should we do if we go the wrong way?
Organiser: Go back to where you were and carry on.
Participant 2: Excuse me, what if we want to give up half-way through?
Organiser: In that case, give your name to a nearby organiser and go home. OK, it's time to start.

…………………………………………………………

Suzuki: Mr. Miller, how was the marathon?
Miller: I came second.
Suzuki: You were second? That's amazing, isn't it?
Miller: No, I'm disappointed that I couldn't win even though I practised hard.
Suzuki: You'll get another chance next year, you know.

## III. Useful Words & Information

### 病院（びょういん） At the Hospital

みんなの病院（びょういん）

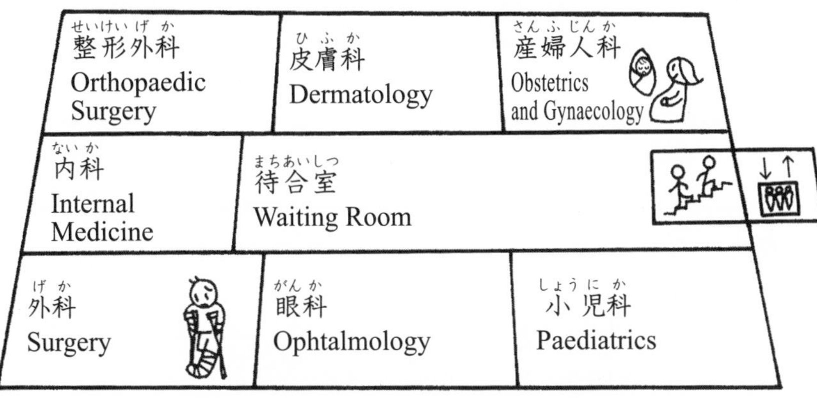


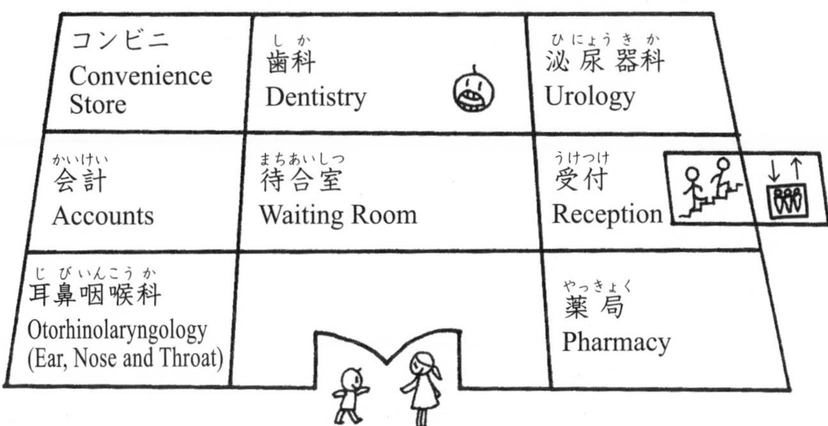


| | |
|---|---|
| 診察（しんさつ）する | examine |
| 検査（けんさ）する | scan, test |
| 注射（ちゅうしゃ）する | inject |
| レントゲンを撮（と）る | take an X-ray |
| 入院（にゅういん）／退院（たいいん）する | be admitted to/be discharged from hospital |
| 手術（しゅじゅつ）する | operate |
| 麻酔（ますい）する | anaesthetise |

| | |
|---|---|
| 処方箋（しょほうせん） | prescription |
| カルテ | patient's chart |
| 保険証（ほけんしょう） | insurance card |
| 診察券（しんさつけん） | patient's registration ticket |

薬（くすり）の種類（しゅるい） types of medicine

痛（いた）み止（ど）め／湿布薬（しっぷやく）／解熱剤（げねつざい）
painkillers/analgesic plasters/antipyretics

錠剤（じょうざい）／粉薬（こなぐすり）／カプセル
tablets (pills)/powders/capsules

## IV. Grammar Notes

**1.**

<table>
<tr><td>V dictionary form</td><td rowspan="6">場合(ばあい)は、～</td></tr>
<tr><td>V ない -form ない</td></tr>
<tr><td>V た -form</td></tr>
<tr><td>い -adj (～い)</td></tr>
<tr><td>な -adj な</td></tr>
<tr><td>N の</td></tr>
</table>

～ばあい is an expression used for postulating a situation. The sentence that follows it indicates how to cope with the situation or its consequences. Since ばあい is a noun, it is connected in the same way as a noun modifier:

① 会議(かいぎ)に 間(ま)に 合(あ)わない 場合(ばあい)は、連絡(れんらく)して ください。

Please contact us if you can't get to the meeting on time.

② 時間(じかん)に 遅(おく)れた 場合(ばあい)は、会場(かいじょう)に 入(はい)れません。

If you are late, you will not be allowed into the venue.

③ パソコンの 調子(ちょうし)が 悪(わる)い 場合(ばあい)は、どう したら いいですか。

What should I do if my PC isn't working properly?

④ 領収書(りょうしゅうしょ)が 必要(ひつよう)な 場合(ばあい)は、言(い)って ください。

Please let me know if you need a receipt.

⑤ 火事(かじ)や 地震(じしん)の 場合(ばあい)は、エレベーターを 使(つか)わないで ください。

Please do not use the lifts in the event of a fire or earthquake.

**2.**

<table>
<tr><td>V</td><td rowspan="2">plain form</td><td rowspan="4">のに、～</td></tr>
<tr><td>い -adj</td></tr>
<tr><td>な -adj</td><td rowspan="2">plain form<br>～だ→～な</td></tr>
<tr><td>N</td></tr>
</table>

のに is used when what is stated in the second clause of a sentence contradicts what would have been expected from the first clause. In most cases, it conveys a feeling of surprise or dissatisfaction:

⑥ 約束(やくそく)を したのに、彼女(かのじょ)は 来(き)ませんでした。

Even though we had a date, she didn't turn up.

⑦ きょうは 日曜日(にちようび)なのに、働(はたら)かなければ なりません。

I have to work today, despite the fact that it's a Sunday.

Example ⑥ expresses the feeling of surprise and disappointment that what had naturally been expected (that she would turn up) from the first clause ('we had a date') had not happened. Example ⑦ uses のに to express a feeling of dissatisfaction that the speaker has had to work, even though the first clause (which states that it is a Sunday) would naturally lead to the conclusion that he or she would be able to have a holiday.

[Note 1] The difference between ～のに and ～が :
If the のに in Examples ⑥ and ⑦ were replaced by が, they would no longer express a feeling of surprise or dissatisfaction:

⑧ 約束(やくそく)を しましたが、彼女(かのじょ)は 来(き)ませんでした。
We had a date, and she didn't turn up.

⑨ きょうは 日曜日(にちようび)ですが、働(はたら)かなければ なりません。
It's Sunday today, and I have to work.

[Note 2] The difference between ～のに and ～ても :
～のに expresses the speaker's feelings about something that has actually happened; it cannot be used like the conjunction ～ても to express a contradictory conclusion in a hypothetical situation:

⑩ あした 雨(あめ)が 降(ふ)っても、サッカーを します。
We're going to play soccer tomorrow even if it rains.

×あした 雨(あめ)が 降(ふ)るのに、サッカーを します。

# Lesson 46

## I. Vocabulary

| | | |
|---|---|---|
| わたします I | 渡します | hand over |
| かえって きますⅢ | 帰って 来ます | come back |
| でますⅡ<br>［バスが～］ | 出ます | [a bus] leave, depart |
| とどきます I<br>［にもつが～］ | 届きます<br>［荷物が～］ | [parcels] be delivered |
| にゅうがくしますⅢ<br>［だいがくに～］ | 入学します<br>［大学に～］ | enter [a university] |
| そつぎょうしますⅢ<br>［だいがくを～］ | 卒業します<br>［大学を～］ | graduate [from a university] |
| やきます I | 焼きます | bake, grill, roast |
| やけますⅡ<br>［パンが～］<br>［にくが～］ | 焼けます<br><br>［肉が～］ | <br>[bread] be baked<br>[meat] be roasted, be grilled |
| るす | 留守 | absence |
| たくはいびん | 宅配便 | （package delivered by）home delivery service |
| げんいん | 原因 | cause |
| こちら | | my side |
| ～の ところ | ～の 所 | where ～ is/are, by the ～ |
| はんとし | 半年 | half a year |
| ちょうど | | just, exactly |
| たったいま | たった今 | just now（used with the past tense; indicates completion） |
| いま いいですか。 | 今 いいですか。 | Have you got a moment? |

**〈会話（かいわ）〉**

| | |
|---|---|
| ガスサービスセンター | gas service centre |
| ガスレンジ | gas range, gas cooker |
| 具合（ぐあい） | condition |
| 申（もう）し訳（わけ）ありません。 | I'm sorry. |
| どちら様（さま）でしょうか。 | Who is this, please? |
| お待（ま）たせしました。 | Sorry to have kept you waiting. |
| 向（む）かいますⅠ | head for |

**〈読（よ）み物（もの）〉**

| | |
|---|---|
| ついて いますⅡ | be lucky |
| 床（ゆか） | floor |
| 転（ころ）びますⅠ | fall down, fall over |
| ベル | bell |
| 鳴（な）りますⅠ | ring |
| 慌（あわ）てて | in a hurry |
| 順番（じゅんばん）に | in order |
| 出来事（できごと） | incident |

## II. Translation

### Sentence Patterns

1. The meeting is about to start.
2. He just graduated from university this March.
3. Mr. Miller must be in the meeting room.

### Example Sentences

1. Hello, Tanaka here. Can I talk to you for a moment?
   ……I'm sorry, I'm just about to get on a train.
   I'll call you back later.
2. Have you found the cause of the breakdown?
   ……No, we're investigating it at the moment.
3. Is Ms. Watanabe here?
   ……Oh, she's just left.
   She might still be by the lifts.
4. How's your work going?
   ……I only joined the company last month, so I don't really know yet.
5. I only bought this video camera last month, and it's already stopped working.
   ……I see. Please let me take a look at it.
6. Hasn't Mr. Miller arrived yet?
   ……He phoned from the station earlier, so he should be here soon.



### Conversation

**I had it fixed only last week, but [it's gone wrong] again......**

Agent: Yes? Gas Service Centre here.
Thawaphon: Err...there's something wrong with my gas cooker.
Agent: What's the matter with it?
Thawaphon: The flame still goes out, even though I had it fixed only last week. It's dangerous, so could you please come and take a look at it soon?
Agent: I understand. I think someone can be with you at around 5:00 pm. Please give me your name and address.

…………………………………………………………

Thawaphon: Hello, someone was supposed to come and look at my gas cooker at about 5:00 pm, but they still haven't come.
Agent: I'm sorry. Who is this, please?
Thawaphon: My name's Thawaphon.
Agent: Just a moment, please. I'll contact the repairman.

…………………………………………………………

Agent: Sorry to have kept you waiting. He's on his way.
He should be there in another ten minutes or so.

## III. Useful Words & Information

### かたかな語のルーツ　　Origins of Katakana Words

Many foreign loanwords have been adopted into the Japanese language, and they are written in katakana. While most katakana words come from English, some come from French, Dutch, German, Portuguese and other languages. The Japanese also create their own katakana words based on foreign words.

| | 食べ物・飲み物<br>Food and Drink | 服飾<br>Clothes and Accessories | 医療関係<br>Medical | 芸術<br>Arts | その他<br>Misc. |
|---|---|---|---|---|---|
| 英語 | ジャム　ハム<br>jam　ham<br>クッキー<br>cookie<br>チーズ<br>cheese | エプロン<br>apron<br>スカート<br>skirt<br>スーツ<br>suit | インフルエンザ<br>influenza<br>ストレス<br>stress | ドラマ<br>drama<br>コーラス<br>chorus<br>メロディー<br>melody | スケジュール<br>schedule<br>ティッシュペーパー<br>tissue paper<br>トラブル　レジャー<br>trouble　leisure |
| フランス語 | コロッケ<br>croquette<br>オムレツ<br>omelette | ズボン<br>trousers<br>ランジェリー<br>lingerie | | バレエ<br>ballet<br>アトリエ<br>studio | アンケート<br>questionnaire<br>コンクール<br>competition |
| ドイツ語 | フランクフルト<br>［ソーセージ］<br>frankfurter | | レントゲン<br>X-ray<br>アレルギー<br>allergy | メルヘン<br>fairy tale | アルバイト<br>part-time job<br>エネルギー<br>energy<br>テーマ<br>theme, topic |
| オランダ語 | ビール<br>beer<br>コーヒー<br>coffee | ホック<br>hook<br>ズック<br>deck shoes, plimsolls | メス<br>scalpel<br>ピンセット<br>tweezers | オルゴール<br>musical box | ゴム　ペンキ<br>rubber　paint<br>ガラス<br>glass |
| ポルトガル語 | パン<br>bread<br>カステラ<br>sponge cake | ビロード<br>velvet<br>ボタン<br>button | | | カルタ<br>playing card |
| イタリア語 | マカロニ　パスタ<br>macaroni　pasta<br>スパゲッティ<br>spaghetti | | | オペラ<br>opera | |

## IV. Grammar Notes

**1.**

| | |
|---|---|
| **V dictionary form**<br>**V て -form いる**<br>**V た -form** | ところです |

The ところ introduced in this lesson is used when describing an aspect of an action or event.

1） V dictionary form　ところです

This indicates that an action is just about to begin. It is often used with adverbs such as これから, [ちょうど] いまから, etc:

① 昼ごはんは　もう　食べましたか。
……いいえ、これから　食べる　ところです。
Have you had lunch yet?
…… No, I was just about to.

② 会議は　もう　始まりましたか。
……いいえ、今から　始まる　ところです。
Has the meeting already started?
…… No, it's just about to.

2） V て -form いる　ところです

This indicates that an action is in progress. It is often used together with いま:

③ 故障の　原因が　わかりましたか。
……いいえ、今　調べて　いる　ところです。
Do you know what caused the breakdown?
…… No, we're investigating it now.

3） V た -form ところです

This indicates that an action has just been completed. It is often used with an adverb such as たったいま:

④ 渡辺さんは　いますか。
……あ、たった今　帰った　ところです。
Is Ms. Watanabe here?
…… Oh, she's just gone home.

⑤ たった今　バスが　出た　ところです。
The bus has just left.

[Note] ～ところです can be connected to various sentence patterns as a nominal clause:

⑥ もしもし　田中ですが、今　いいでしょうか。
……すみません。今から　出かける　ところなんです。
Hello, Tanaka here. Have you got a moment?
…… Sorry, I'm just going out.

## 2. V た -form ばかりです

This sentence pattern also expresses the speaker's sense that not much time has passed since an action has been performed or an event has occurred. However, unlike V た -form ところです , this sentence pattern can be used regardless of how much time has elapsed if the speaker feels it is short:

⑦ さっき 昼(ひる)ごはんを 食(た)べた ばかりです。

I've only just had lunch.

⑧ 木村(きむら)さんは 先月(せんげつ) この 会社(かいしゃ)に 入(はい)った ばかりです。

Ms. Kimura only joined the company last month.

[Note] ～ばかりです can also be attached to various sentence patterns as a nominal clause:

⑨ この ビデオは 先週(せんしゅう) 買(か)った ばかりなのに、調子(ちょうし)が おかしいです。

This video isn't working properly, even though I only bought it last month.

## 3.

| | |
|---|---|
| **V dictionary form**<br>**V ない -form ない**<br>**い -adj (～い)**<br>**な -adj な**<br>**N の** | はずです |

This sentence pattern is used when a speaker is decisively stating a conclusion that he or she has reached based on particular grounds:

⑩ ミラーさんは きょう 来(く)るでしょうか。

……来(く)る はずですよ。きのう 電話(でんわ)が ありましたから。

Will Mr. Miller come today, I wonder?

…… He's bound to come. He (said so when he) called yesterday.

In Example ⑩ , 'He called yesterday' is the basis for the speaker's conclusion that Mr. Miller will come today, and the speaker uses ～はずです to convey the certainty he or she feels about the correctness of that conclusion.

# Lesson 47

47

## I. Vocabulary

| | | |
|---|---|---|
| ふきますⅠ［かぜが～］ | 吹きます［風が～］ | [wind] blow |
| もえますⅡ［ごみが～］ | 燃えます | [rubbish] burn |
| なくなりますⅠ | 亡くなります | pass away (euphemistic equivalent of しにます) |
| あつまりますⅠ［ひとが～］ | 集まります［人が～］ | [people] gather |
| わかれますⅡ［ひとが～］ | 別れます［人が～］ | [people] part, separate |
| しますⅢ | | |
| ［おと／こえが～］ | ［音／声が～］ | [sound/voice] be heard |
| ［あじが～］ | ［味が～］ | taste |
| ［においが～］ | | smell |
| きびしい | 厳しい | strict, hard |
| ひどい | | terrible, severe |
| こわい | 怖い | frightening, horrible |
| じっけん | 実験 | experiment |
| データ | | data |
| じんこう | 人口 | population |
| におい | | smell |
| かがく | 科学 | science |
| いがく* | 医学 | medicine, medical science |
| ぶんがく | 文学 | literature |
| パトカー | | police car |
| きゅうきゅうしゃ | 救急車 | ambulance |
| さんせい | 賛成 | approval, agreement |
| はんたい | 反対 | objection, opposition |
| だいとうりょう | 大統領 | president |
| ～に よると | | according to ～ (indicates that the source of information) |

**〈会話〉**

| | |
|---|---|
| 婚約します III | get engaged |
| どうも | it seems that (used when making a tentative judgement) |
| 恋人 | sweetheart, boyfriend, girlfriend |
| 相手 | the other person |
| 知り合います I | get acquainted |

**〈読み物〉**

| | |
|---|---|
| 化粧 | makeup (～を します：put on makeup) |
| 世話を します III | take care of |
| 女性 | female, woman |
| 男性 | male, man |
| 長生き | long life (～します：live long) |
| 理由 | reason |
| 関係 | relationship |

## II. Translation

47

### Sentence Patterns

1. According to the weather forecast, it's going to be cold tomorrow.
2. There seems to be somebody in the next room.

### Example Sentences

1. The newspaper says that there's going to be a Japanese speech competition in January. Wouldn't you like to enter it, Mr Miller?
   ……Hmm... I'll think about it.
2. I heard that Klara lived in France when she was a child.
   ……That's why she understands French too, isn't it?
3. They say that Power Electric's new electronic dictionary is very good and easy to use.
   ……Yes it is; I've already bought one.
4. They say Professor Watt is a strict teacher, don't they?
   ……Yes, but his lessons are very interesting.
5. They're lively, aren't they?
   ……Yes, it sounds like they're having a party or something.
6. There are a lot of people, aren't there?
   ……It looks like there's been an accident. Some police cars and an ambulance have turned up.



### Conversation

**She got engaged, apparently**

Watanabe: I'm off now. Goodbye. (lit: Excuse me for leaving before you).
Takahashi: Oh, Ms. Watanabe, wait a moment. I'm going home, too.
Watanabe: Sorry, I'm in a bit of a hurry.

………………………………………………………

Takahashi: Ms. Watanabe leaves early these days, doesn't she?
It looks like she's found herself a sweetheart, doesn't it?
Hayashi: Oh, didn't you know? Apparently, she got engaged recently.
Takahashi: Really? Who to?
Hayashi: Mr. Suzuki from IMC.
Takahashi: Really? Mr. Suzuki?
Hayashi: It seems they met at Professor Watt's wedding.
Takahashi: Did they?
Hayashi: By the way, how about you, Mr. Takahashi?
Takahashi: Me? My work is my sweetheart.

## III. Useful Words & Information

### 擬音語・擬態語　　Onomatopoeia

ザーザー（降る）
pour, crash (rain)
ピューピュー（吹く）
whistle, howl (wind)
ゴロゴロ（鳴る）
roll, growl (thunder)
ワンワン（ほえる）
bow-wow
ニャーニャー（鳴く）
meow
カーカー（鳴く）
caw
げらげら（笑う）
guffaw
しくしく（泣く）
sob
きょろきょろ（見る）
(look around) restlessly
ぱくぱく（食べる）
(eat) heartily, gobble
ぐうぐう（寝る）
be fast asleep
すらすら（読む）
(read) fluently
ざらざら（している）
(feel) rough
べたべた（している）
(be) sticky
つるつる（している）
(be) smooth, slippery

47

## IV. Grammar Notes

### 1. Plain form そうです They say that ～

This is an expression for conveying information from another source without introducing one's own opinion. When the source of the information is given, it is put at the beginning of the sentence and is indicated by ～に よると:

① 天気予報に よると、あしたは 寒く なるそうです。
According to the weather forecast, it will be cold tomorrow.

② クララさんは 子どもの とき、フランスに 住んで いたそうです。
I hear that Klara used to live in France when she was a child.

③ バリは とても きれいだそうです。
They say Bali is very beautiful.

[Note 1] Note that this is different in meaning and construction from the ～そうです introduced in Lesson 43, as illustrated below:

④ 雨が 降りそうです。 It looks like rain. (See Lesson 43)

⑤ 雨が 降るそうです。 I heard that it's going to rain.

⑥ この 料理は おいしそうです。 This food looks delicious. (See Lesson 43)

⑦ この 料理は おいしいそうです。They say this food is delicious.

[Note 2] The difference between ～そうです (hearsay) and ～と いって いました (see Lesson 33):

⑧ ミラーさんは あした 京都へ 行くそうです。
Apparently, Mr. Miller is going to Kyoto tomorrow.

⑨ ミラーさんは あした 京都へ 行くと 言って いました。
Mr. Miller said he was going to Kyoto tomorrow.

While in Example ⑨, Mr. Miller himself is the information source, in Example ⑧, the information source may be someone or something other than Mr. Miller.

### 2.

| | | |
|---|---|---|
| V<br>い-adj | plain form | ようです |
| な-adj | plain form ～だ→～な | |
| N | plain form ～だ→～の | |

It seems that ～

～ようです is an expression used to describe what the speaker has concluded from observing a situation. It is sometimes used with the adverb どうも when the speaker wishes to emphasise the tentative nature of his or her conclusion:

⑩ 人が 大勢 集まって いますね。
……事故のようですね。パトカーと 救急車が 来て いますよ。
There's a big crowd here, isn't there?
…… It looks like there may have been an accident. A police car and an ambulance have arrived.

⑪ せきも 出るし、頭も 痛い。どうも かぜを ひいたようだ。
I've got a cough, and my head aches. I think I might have caught a cold.

[Note] The difference between ～そうです (Lesson 43) and ～ようです

⑫　ミラーさんは 忙(いそが)しそうです。　Mr. Miller looks busy.

⑬　ミラーさんは 忙(いそが)しいようです。Mr. Miller seems to be busy.

While Example ⑫ merely describes Mr. Miller's external appearance, Example ⑬ expresses a conclusion that the speaker has arrived at based on his or her observations (e.g. that Mr. Miller is difficult to contact, or that he did not come to a party that he had said he would come to).

### 3. 声(こえ)／音(おと)／におい／味(あじ)が します

⑭　にぎやかな 声(こえ)が しますね。

They're talking excitedly, aren't they? [Lit: There are some lively voices, aren't there?]

This describes a voice, other sound, smell, taste or other sensation that the speaker has perceived using his or her sense organs.

# Lesson 48

## I. Vocabulary

48

| | | |
|---|---|---|
| おろします I | 降ろします、<br>下ろします | put down, lower, unload |
| とどけます II | 届けます | deliver |
| せわを します III | 世話を します | take care of |
| ろくおんします III | 録音します | record |
| いや[な] | 嫌[な] | unwilling, reluctant |
| じゅく | 塾 | cram school |
| せいと | 生徒 | pupil |
| ファイル | | file |
| じゆうに | 自由に | freely |
| ～かん | ～間 | for ～ (referring to duration) |
| いい ことですね。 | | That's good. |

48

**〈会話(かいわ)〉**

| | |
|---|---|
| お忙(いそが)しいですか。 | Are you busy? (used when talking to someone senior or older) |
| 営業(えいぎょう) | business, sales |
| それまでに | by that time |
| かまいません。 | It's all right./I don't mind. |
| 楽(たの)しみます I | enjoy oneself |

**〈読(よ)み物(もの)〉**

| | |
|---|---|
| 親(おや) | parent |
| 小学生(しょうがくせい) | pupil, elementary schoolchild |
| ーパーセント | ー percent |
| その次(つぎ) | next |
| 習字(しゅうじ) | calligraphy |
| 普通(ふつう)の | normal, usual |

## II. Translation

### Sentence Patterns

1. I'm sending my son to the UK to study.
2. I'm going to get my daughter to learn the piano.

### Example Sentences

1. They say they practise hard in this soccer class, don't they?
   ……Yes, they make the children run a kilometre every day.
2. It's time I was going.
   ……Oh, wait a moment please. I'll get my son to take you to the station.
3. Is Hans learning anything else apart from what he studies at school?
   ……Yes, he said he wanted to do judo, so we're sending him to a judo class.
4. What's Ms. Ito like as a teacher?
   ……She's a good teacher. She lets her pupils read the books they like, and gives them the freedom to say what they think.
5. Excuse me, would it be all right if I parked my car here for a little while?
   ……Yes, that would be fine.

### Conversation

**I wondered if I might take a holiday?**

| | |
|---|---|
| Miller: | Ms. Nakamura, are you busy at the moment? |
| Section Manager Nakamura: | No, go ahead. |
| Miller: | I have a small request...... |
| Section Manager Nakamura: | What is it? |
| Miller: | I wondered if I might take ten days off from the seventh of next month? |
| Section Manager Nakamura: | Ten days? |
| Miller: | Actually, a friend in America is getting married. |
| Section Manager Nakamura: | Really?<br>Let's see...there's a sales meeting on the twentieth of next month, but you can be back by then, can't you? |
| Miller: | Yes. |
| Section Manager Nakamura: | In that case, I don't mind. Have a good time. |
| Miller: | Thank you very much. |

## III. Useful Words & Information

### しつける・鍛える　Discipline

子どもに何をさせますか。　What will you make or let your children do?

- 自然の中で遊ぶ
  play outdoors in natural surroundings
- スポーツをする
  do sports
- 一人で旅行する
  go on a trip alone
- いろいろな経験をする
  have various experiences

- いい本をたくさん読む
  read many good books
- お年寄りの話を聞く
  listen to old people

- ボランティアに参加する
  participate in voluntary activities
- うちの仕事を手伝う
  do household chores
- 弟や妹、おじいちゃん、おばあちゃんの世話をする
  take care of their younger brothers, younger sisters, grandfathers and grandmothers
- 自分がやりたいことをやる
  do what they want to do

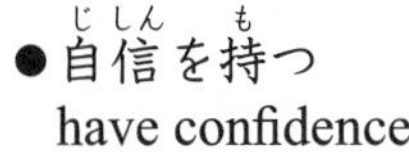

- 自分のことは自分で決める
  make decisions by themselves

- 自信を持つ
  have confidence
- 責任を持つ
  take responsibility
- 我慢する
  be patient

- 塾へ行く
  go to cram school
- ピアノや英語を習う
  learn to play the piano, learn English and so on

# IV. Grammar Notes

## 1. Causative verbs

| | | Causative verbs | |
|---|---|---|---|
| | | Polite form | Plain form |
| I | いきます | いかせます | いかせる |
| II | たべます | たべさせます | たべさせる |
| III | きます<br>します | こさせます<br>させます | こさせる<br>させる |

(See Exercise A1, Lesson 48, Main Text)

Causative verbs are conjugated as Group II verbs.

Examples: かかせます　　かかせる　　かかせ(ない)　　かかせて

## 2. Causative-verb sentences

With some causative verbs, the subject of the action is indicated by を, while with others it is indicated by に. In principle, if the base verb is intransitive, を is used as in 1) below, while if it is transitive, に is used as in 2) below.

1) N(person)を causative verb(intransitive)　　make/let a person verb(intransitive)

① 部長は ミラーさんを アメリカへ 出張させます。

The Department Manager makes Mr. Miller go to America on business.

② わたしは 娘を 自由に 遊ばせました。

I allowed my daughter to play freely.

[Note] When an intransitive verb with 'N (place) を' is used in the sentence, the subject of the action is indicated by に:

③ わたしは 子どもに 道の 右側を 歩かせます。

I make my children walk on the right-hand side of the road.

2) $N_1$(person)に $N_2$を causative verb(transitive)　　make/let a person verb(transitive)

④ 朝は 忙しいですから、娘に 朝ごはんの 準備を 手伝わせます。

I'm busy in the mornings, so I get my daughter to help me prepare breakfast.

⑤ 先生は 生徒に 自由に 意見を 言わせました。

The teacher allowed his pupils to express their opinions freely.

## 3. How to use causative verbs

Causative verbs indicate compulsion or permission. For example, they are used by someone of higher status to someone of lower status (e.g. a parent to a child, an older brother to a younger brother, or a manager to his team members) to compel or permit the latter to do something. Examples ①, ③ and ④ are examples of compulsion, while Examples ② and ⑤ are examples of permission.

[Note] Someone of inferior status would not normally use a causative verb in relation to their superior, because someone inferior is not in the position of being able to compel or permit their superior to do anything. To express having someone of superior status do something (e.g. ぶちょう and せつめいします in Example ⑥ below), the speaker uses a phrase designed to show that he or she has received a favour, such as V て-form いただきます and V て-form もらいます. This usage can also be employed when the speaker wishes to indicate that he or she has received a favour or benefit from someone of equal or inferior status, as in Example ⑦ below:

⑥ わたしは 部長(ぶちょう)に 説明(せつめい)して いただきました。
　I had it explained to me by the Department Manager.

⑦ わたしは 友達(ともだち)に 説明(せつめい)して もらいました。
　I had it explained to me by a friend.

## 4. **Causative verb て-form いただけませんか** Would you please let me do ～?

V て-form いただけませんか was introduced in Lesson 26 as a very polite way of asking someone to do something. Causative verb て-form いただけませんか is used when politely asking the listener to allow one to do something:

⑧ いい 先生(せんせい)を 紹介(しょうかい)して いただけませんか。
　Would you be kind enough to introduce me to a good teacher? (see Lesson 26)

⑨ 友達(ともだち)の 結婚式(けっこんしき)が あるので、早(はや)く 帰(かえ)らせて いただけませんか。
　I'm going to a friend's wedding, so would you mind letting me leave early?

In Example ⑧ it is the listener who is being asked to do the introducing ( しょうかいします ), while in Example ⑨ it is the speaker who is asking to be allowed to leave ( かえります ) early.

# Lesson 49

## I. Vocabulary

| | | |
|---|---|---|
| りようしますⅢ | 利用します | use |
| つとめますⅡ<br>［かいしゃに～］ | 勤めます<br>［会社に～］ | work [for a company] |
| かけますⅡ<br>［いすに～］ | 掛けます | sit on [a chair] |
| すごしますⅠ | 過ごします | spend (time), pass (time) |
| いらっしゃいますⅠ | | be, go, come (respectful equivalent of います, いきます and きます) |
| めしあがりますⅠ | 召し上がります | eat, drink (respectful equivalent of たべます and のみます) |
| おっしゃいますⅠ | | say, (one's name) is ～ (respectful equivalent of いいます) |
| なさいますⅠ | | do (respectful equivalent of します) |
| ごらんに なりますⅠ | ご覧に なります | see, look at (respectful equivalent of みます) |
| ごぞんじです | ご存じです | know (respectful equivalent of しって います) |
| | | |
| あいさつ | | greeting, address (～を します: greet, give an address) |
| | | |
| りょかん | 旅館 | Japanese-style hotel or inn |
| バスてい | バス停 | bus stop |
| | | |
| おくさま | 奥様 | (someone else's) wife (respectful equivalent of おくさん) |
| ～さま | ～様 | (respectful equivalent of ～さん) |
| | | |
| たまに | | once in a while |
| どなたでも | | anybody (respectful equivalent of だれでも) |
| | | |
| ～と いいます | | (one's name) is ～ |

**〈会話〉**

| | |
|---|---|
| －年－組 | class － of -th grade |
| 出しますⅠ ［熱を～］ | run [a fever] |
| よろしく お伝え ください。 | Give my best regards./Please say hello. |
| 失礼いたします。 | Goodbye.（humble equivalent of しつれいします） |
| ※ひまわり小学校 | fictitious elementary school |

**〈読み物〉**

| | |
|---|---|
| 経歴 | background |
| 医学部 | the medical department |
| 目指しますⅠ | aim for |
| 進みますⅠ | go on（to graduate school） |
| iPS細胞 | induced pluripotent stem cell |
| 開発しますⅢ | develop, create |
| マウス | mouse |
| ヒト | human |
| 受賞しますⅢ | be awarded a prize |
| 講演会 | lecture meeting |
| ※山中伸弥 | Japanese medical scientist（1962- ） |
| ※ノーベル賞 | Nobel Prize |

## II. Translation

### Sentence Patterns

1. The section manager has gone home.
2. The president has gone home.
3. The department manager is going to America on business.
4. Please wait a little while.

### Example Sentences

1. Did you read this book?
   ……Yes, I've already read it.
2. Where's the department manager?
   ……He went out earlier.
3. Do you often watch films?
   ……Well, I sometimes go to watch one with my wife.
4. Did you know that Mr. Ogawa's son has passed the entrance examination for Sakura University?
   ……No, I didn't.
5. May I ask your name?
   ……My name is Watt.
6. What work do you do?
   ……I'm a bank employee. I work at Apple Bank.
7. Is Department Manager Matsumoto in?
   ……Yes, he's in this room. Please go in.



### Conversation

**Please give her my regards**

Teacher: Hello, Himawari Primary School here.
Klara: Good morning.
I'm the mother of Hans Schmidt of Class 2, Year 5. Could I speak to Ms. Ito, please?
Teacher: She's not here yet, I'm afraid.
Klara: In that case, could you give her a message?
Teacher: Yes, what is it?
Klara: As a matter of fact, Hans had a fever last night, and his temperature hasn't come down yet.
Teacher: I'm sorry to hear that.
Klara: So I'm going to keep him out of school today. Could you tell Ms. Ito, please?
Teacher: I understand. I hope he gets better soon.
Klara: Thank you. Goodbye.

## III. Useful Words & Information

### 季節（きせつ）の行事（ぎょうじ）　Seasonal Events

1月1日（がつついたち）～3日（みっか）

**お正月（しょうがつ）** New Year

Celebration at the beginning of the year. People go to shrines or temples to pray for health and prosperity.

2月3日（がつみっか）ごろ

**豆（まめ）まき** Bean-Scattering Ceremony

On the eve of Setsubun (the last day of winter in the traditional Japanese calendar), people scatter roasted soybeans while shouting, "Devils out, good luck in!"

3月3日（がつみっか）

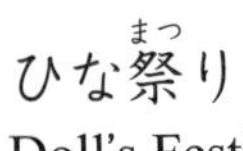

**ひな祭（まつ）り**
Doll's Festival

Families with a daughter create an elaborate display of dolls.

5月5日（がついつか）

**こどもの日（ひ）** Children's day

Celebration for the growth and health of children. Originally, the day was for celebrating the growth of boys, but now it is for boys and girls.

7月7日（がつなのか）

**七夕（たなばた）** Star Festival

Based on a Chinese legend in which Altair and Vega travel from the eastern and western extremes of the Milky Way once a year to meet.

8月（がつ）13日（にち）～15日（にち）

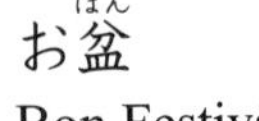

**お盆（ぼん）**
Bon Festival

The Bon Festival is a Buddhist tradition in which people visit the cemetery where their relatives are buried in order to greet the spirits of their deceased ancestors.

9月（がつ）15日（にち）ごろ

**お月見（つきみ）**
Moon Viewing

People enjoy viewing the full moon.

12月（がつ）31日（にち）

**大（おお）みそか** New Year's Eve

People prepare for the New Year, cooking *osechi ryori* (special food for New Year's Day) and cleaning the house. Temple bells are rung at midnight.

# IV. Grammar Notes

## 1. 敬語 (Honorific expressions)

けいご (honorific expressions) are used to show respect to the listener or the person being referred to. Whether or not to use them is determined by who the listener or person referred to is, and the situation. Basically, they are used in situations such as (1) when talking to someone of higher status than oneself, someone one does not know, or someone with whom one is not on familiar terms, (2) when talking about someone of higher status than oneself, and (3) when talking in a formal situation. One type of けいご is そんけいご (respectful expressions), introduced in Lesson 49, and another is けんじょうご (humble expressions), introduced in Lesson 50.

## 2. 尊敬語 (Respectful expressions)

Respectful expressions show respect towards the person performing the action or in the state mentioned.

1) Verbs

These show respect towards the person performing the action indicated by the verb.

(1) Respectful verbs (See Exercise A1, Lesson 49, Main Text)

These take the same form as passive verbs and are conjugated as Group II verbs.

Examples: かかれます　　かかれる　　かかれ(ない)　　かかれて

① 中村さんは 7時に 来られます。 Ms. Nakamura is coming at 7 o'clock.

② お酒を やめられたんですか。 Have you given up drinking?

(2) おVます-form に なります

This form is generally considered to be more polite than the respectful verbs introduced in (1). Group III verbs and verbs whose ます-form consists of one syllable, such as みます and ねます, do not have this form. If a verb has a respectful equivalent such as those featured in (3) below, this is used.

③ 社長は もう お帰りに なりました。

The company president has already gone home.

(3) Special respectful verbs (See Exercise A4, Lesson 49, Main Text)

Several verbs have special respectful equivalents, which show a level of respect similar to (2):

④ ワット先生は 研究室に いらっしゃいます。

Professor Watt is in his office.

⑤ どうぞ 召し上がって ください。 Please go ahead.

[Note 1] いらっしゃいます (dictionary form: いらっしゃる), なさいます (dictionary form: なさる, くださいます (dictionary form: くださる) and おっしゃいます (dictionary form: おっしゃる) are Group I verbs, and care must be taken over their conjugation.

Example: いらっしゃいます (×いらっしゃります)　　いらっしゃる
いらっしゃらない　　いらっしゃった　　いらっしゃらなかった

(4) お／ご～ ください

This sentence pattern is the respectful equivalent of Vて-form ください (see Lesson 14). Verbs in Groups I and II take the form おVます-form ください, while Group III verbs (N します) take the form ごN ください.

⑥ どうぞ お入り ください。

Please come in.

⑦ 忘れ物に ご注意 ください。

Please take care not to leave anything behind.

Verbs such as みます and ねます whose ます -forms have only one syllable do not use this form. When a verb has a special respectful equivalent such as those featured in (3), the respectful equivalent's て -form with ください attached is used.

⑧ また いらっしゃって ください。

Please come again.

2) Nouns, adjectives and adverbs

お or ご is prefixed to nouns, adjectives and adverbs in order to signify respect towards the possessor of the thing represented by the noun or the person in the state described by the adjective or adverb. Whether to use お or ご depends on the word to which it is to be prefixed; as a general rule, お is prefixed to uniquely Japanese words, and ご to words of Chinese origin.

| Examples of words prefixed by お | | Examples of words prefixed by ご | |
|---|---|---|---|
| Nouns | お国, お名前, お仕事<br>お約束, お電話 | Nouns | ご家族, ご意見, ご旅行 |
| な -adj | お元気, お上手, お暇 | な -adj | ご熱心, ご親切 |
| い -adj | お忙しい, お若い | adverb | ご自由に |

[Note 2] けいご are often used not just with verbs but also with other words in a sentence:

⑨ 部長の 奥様も ごいっしょに ゴルフに 行かれます。

The Department Manager's wife also goes to play golf with him.



## 3. Honorific expressions and sentence style

When expressing respect towards someone being talked about, in a case where there is no need to do so towards the listener, けいご can be used in a plain-style sentence as in Example ⑩:

⑩ 部長は 何時に いらっしゃる? What time will the Department Manager arrive?

## 4. ～まして

When wishing to speak politely, V て -form may be changed to V ます -form まして.

⑪ ハンスが ゆうべ 熱を 出しまして、けさも まだ 下がらないんです。

Hans started running a temperature last night, and this morning it still hasn't gone down.

## 5. ～ますので

Polite form ので may be used in order to make plain form ので more polite.

⑫ きょうは 学校を 休ませますので、先生に よろしく お伝え ください。

I'm keeping him out of school today; please give my regards to his teacher.

# Lesson 50



## I. Vocabulary

| | | |
|---|---|---|
| まいります I | 参ります | go, come (humble equivalent of いきます and きます) |
| おります I | | be (humble equivalent of います) |
| いただきます I | | eat, drink, receive (humble equivalent of たべます, のみます and もらいます) |
| もうします I | 申します | say, (one's name) is ～ (humble equivalent of いいます) |
| いたします I | | do (humble equivalent of します) |
| はいけんします III | 拝見します | see (humble equivalent of みます) |
| ぞんじます II | 存じます | get to know (humble equivalent of しります) |
| うかがいます I | 伺います | ask, hear, visit (humble equivalent of ききます and いきます) |
| おめに かかります I | お目に かかります | meet (humble equivalent of あいます) |
| いれます II [コーヒーを～] | | make [coffee] |
| よういします III | 用意します | prepare |
| わたくし | 私 | I (humble equivalent of わたし) |
| ガイド | | guide |
| メールアドレス | | e-mail address |
| スケジュール | | schedule |
| さらいしゅう* | さ来週 | the week after next |
| さらいげつ | さ来月 | the month after next |
| さらいねん* | さ来年 | the year after next |
| はじめに | 初めに | first |
| ※江戸東京博物館（えどとうきょうはくぶつかん） | | Edo-Tokyo Museum |

**〈会話(かいわ)〉**

| | |
|---|---|
| 緊張(きんちょう)しますⅢ | become tense, be strained, be nervous |
| 賞金(しょうきん) | prize money |
| きりん | giraffe |
| ころ | times, days |
| かないますⅠ ［夢(ゆめ)が～］ | [dream] be realized, come true |
| 応援(おうえん)しますⅢ | support |
| 心(こころ)から | from one's heart, sincerely |
| 感謝(かんしゃ)しますⅢ | thank, be greatful |

**〈読(よ)み物(もの)〉**

| | |
|---|---|
| お礼(れい) | gratitude, thanks |
| お元気(げんき)で いらっしゃいますか。 | How are you doing? (respectful equivalent of おげんきですか) |
| 迷惑(めいわく)を かけますⅡ | cause trouble, annoyance, inconvenience |
| 生(い)かしますⅠ | make good use of |
| ※ミュンヘン | Munich (in Germany) |

## II. Translation

### Sentence Patterns

1. I'll send you this month's schedule.
2. I'll come at three o'clock tomorrow.
3. I'm from America.

### Example Sentences

1. That looks heavy. Shall I carry it for you?
   ……Thank you. Yes, please.
2. Guide, where are we going after we've seen this?
   ……I'm taking you to the Edo-Tokyo Museum.
3. Mr. Gupta is arriving at two o'clock, isn't he? Is anyone going to pick him up?
   ……Yes, I am.
4. May I see your ticket a moment?
   ……Yes.
   Thank you very much.
5. This is Mr. Miller.
   ……How do you do. My name is Miller.
   Nice to meet you.
6. Where's your family?
   ……They're in New York.

### Conversation

**I'm sincerely grateful**

MC: Congratulations on winning.
It was an excellent speech.
Miller: Thank you.
MC: Were you nervous?
Miller: Yes, very.
MC: Was practising tough?
Miller: Yes, I was busy, and I didn't have much time to practise.
MC: What will you spend your prize money on?
Miller: Hmm...I love animals, and it was my childhood dream to go to Africa.
MC: So will you be going there?
Miller: Yes. I'd like to see giraffes, elephants and other animals in the wild there.
MC: So your childhood dream will come true, won't it?
Miller: Yes. I'm very happy.
I'm sincerely grateful to everyone who supported me.
Thank you very much.

## III. Useful Words & Information

### 封筒・はがきのあて名の書き方　How to Write Addresses

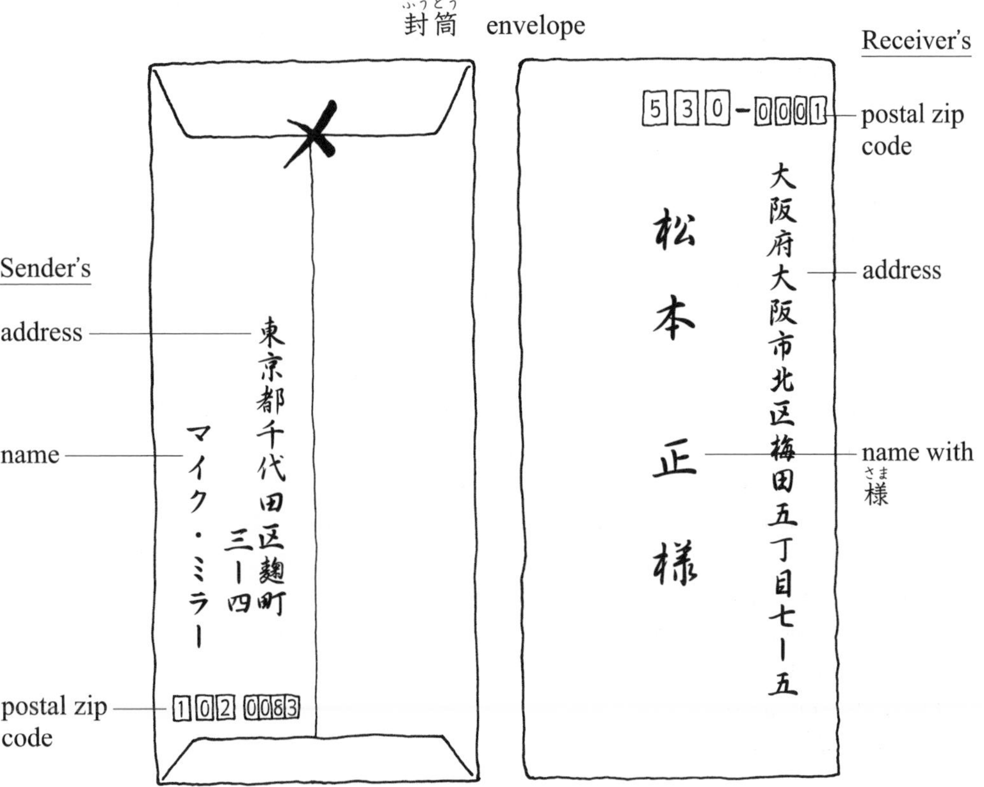


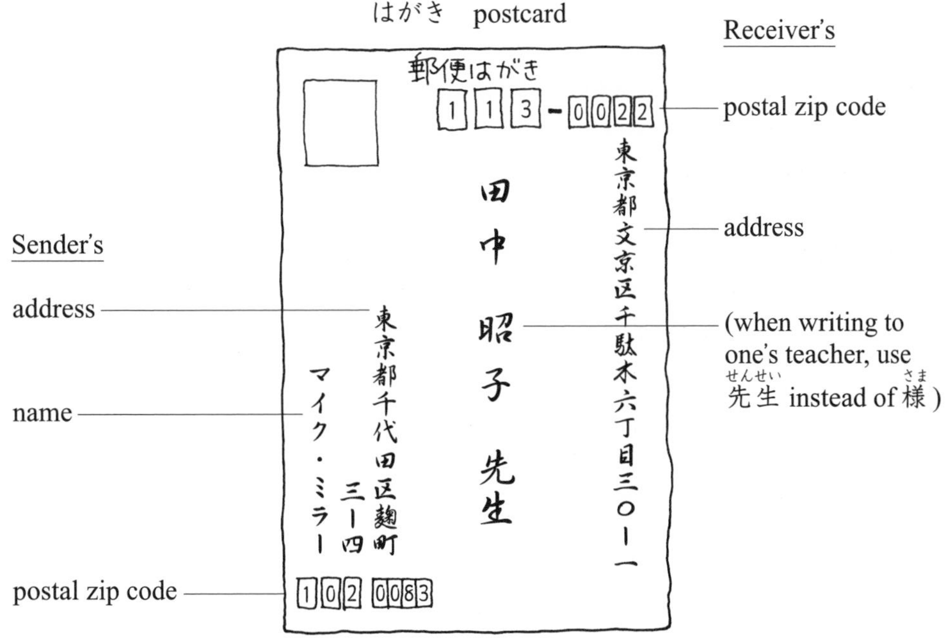


50

## IV. Grammar Notes



### 1. 謙譲語Ⅰ（Humble expressions I - verbs）

Humble expressions I are expressions that humbly refer to the actions of the speaker or someone associated with the speaker in order to show respect to the person towards which those actions are directed (who may or may not be the listener).

1）お／ご～します

（1）おV（Group I or II）ます-formします

① 重そうですね。お持ちしましょうか。

That looks heavy; may I carry it for you?

② 私が 社長に スケジュールを お知らせします。

I will tell the president about the schedule.

③ 兄が 車で お送りします。　　My elder brother will take you in his car.

In Example ①, the speaker is showing respect to the person attempting to carry the heavy item referred to (who, in this case, happens to be the person the speaker is addressing). In Example ②, the speaker is showing respect to the person to whom the action 'tell' is to be directed (i.e. the president, in this case). In Example ③, the speaker is showing respect to the person who is to be taken in the car (who, in this case, happens to be the person the speaker is addressing).

This form cannot be used with verbs whose ます-form consists of a single syllable, such as みます and います.

（2）ごV（Group III）

④ 江戸東京博物館へ ご案内します。

I will take you to the Edo-Tokyo Museum.

⑤ きょうの 予定を ご説明します。

I will explain today's schedule.

This form is used with Group III verbs, including verbs such as しょうかいします, しょうたいします, そうだんします and れんらくします in addition to those in the above examples. However, some verbs such as でんわします and やくそくします are exceptions, taking お, not ご.

2）Special humble verbs (See Exercise A3, Lesson 50, Main Text)

A number of verbs have special humble equivalents:

⑥ 社長の 奥様に お目に かかりました。

I met the company president's wife.

⑦ あしたは だれが 手伝いに 来て くれますか。

……私が 伺います。

Who is coming to help tomorrow?

…… I am [coming].

## 2. 謙譲語Ⅱ（Humble expressions II - verbs）

These are used to refer to the actions of the speaker or of his or her associates in a way that shows politeness towards the listener:

⑧　私は ミラーと 申します。　　My name is Miller.

⑨　アメリカから 参りました。　　I come from the United States.

The speaker uses もうします (the humble equivalent of いいます) in Example ⑧, and まいりました (the humble equivalent of きました) in Example ⑨, in order to mention his or her own actions politely to the listener.
Additional humble equivalent include いたします and ［～て］おります.

**監修**　Supervisor
鶴尾能子（Tsuruo Yoshiko）　石沢弘子（Ishizawa Hiroko）

**執筆協力**　Contributors
田中よね（Tanaka Yone）　澤田幸子（Sawada Sachiko）　重川明美（Shigekawa Akemi）
牧野昭子（Makino Akiko）　御子神慶子（Mikogami Keiko）

**英語翻訳**　English translator
John H. Loftus

**本文イラスト**　Illustrator
向井直子（Mukai Naoko）　柴野和香（Shibano Waka）　佐藤夏枝（Sato Natsue）

**装丁・本文デザイン**　Cover and Layout Designer
山田武（Yamada Takeshi）

**みんなの日本語　初級 II　第２版**
**翻訳・文法解説　英語版**

1998年３月16日　初版第１刷発行
2013年12月９日　第２版第１刷発行
2019年７月23日　第２版第８刷発行

編著者　スリーエーネットワーク
発行者　藤嵜政子
発　行　株式会社スリーエーネットワーク
〒102-0083　東京都千代田区麹町３丁目４番
トラスティ麹町ビル２Ｆ
電話　営業　03(5275)2722
編集　03(5275)2725
https://www.3anet.co.jp/
印　刷　倉敷印刷株式会社

ISBN978-4-88319-664-7 C0081